PREGAME

ALCOHOL, ADDICTION &
RECOVERY THROUGH THE EYES
OF A COLLEGE STUDENT

MARGARET E. KING

NEW DEGREE PRESS

COPYRIGHT © 2019 MARGARET E. KING

All rights reserved.

PREGAME

Alcohol, Addiction & Recovery Through the Eyes of a College Student

ISBN   978-1-64137-234-3   *Paperback*

          978-1-64137-235-0   *Ebook*

PREGAME

For each and every one of us living one day at a time.

CONTENTS

PREFACE

———

As a child growing up in the suburbs of Philadelphia, I had anything I ever wanted. Dance lessons, thirteen years in private school, and a financially stable family of four.

Throughout my lower and middle school years, I remember feeling that I was destined to be the best. The inner drive I felt to impress and perform was encouraged in a high- achieving school like mine.

I did achieve.

By the time I graduated high school, I was the captain of the field hockey team, the lead in the school musical, and on my way to a prestigious liberal arts college in Massachusetts.

I had it all.

If you looked at my resume, I was the perfect teen.

But the problem was it wasn't enough.

It never was.

I spent my childhood breaking my neck, gaining accolade after accolade just to continue to feel that I wasn't good enough. I always thought that if I got the grade, won the award, or scored the goal, I would feel better, but I didn't.

I could never keep the same friends for more than a few years because I always thought there was something better. Yet whenever I thought I had reached the goal, it wasn't enough.

When I celebrated my fourteenth birthday, the friends I spent the summer with started talking about getting a case of beer to drink in the woods. I had witnessed family members drunk throughout my life and vowed I would never be like them. I was firmly against drugs and alcohol from the second I witnessed their effects.

When I was a junior in high school, I started seeing the school psychologist. I staged my own intervention with my parents, telling them that I was depressed and needed therapy and medication. I was a closeted queer teen with crippling anxiety and depression. I longed to fit in, to feel "okay." The same year, my mother was diagnosed with breast cancer. I was lost. Any confidence I had built up over the years had been drained from me.

The feeling of being "different" got worse.

* * *

That summer, the anxiety I felt to fit in and be liked by my peers loosened my harsh views on alcohol.

I don't remember my first drink, what it was, or where it was, but I know that the circling thoughts in my head stopped as soon as the drink touched my lips.

There was a rush of confidence, an invincibility that came over me.

I had arrived.

I was sixteen years old and was immediately a blackout drinker. I was the friend that would party every night throughout the summer and every weekend during the school year. If friends wanted to take a night off, I'd offer to drive to the beer distributor. If we were playing a drinking game, I'd win every round. If we were out of alcohol, I'd leave the party and drink alone at home. I was surprised when friends would tell me I should slow down, that I probably shouldn't drink so much as a girl my size. I persisted and met marijuana not too long after.

I never did well with large groups of girls and found myself making more male friends through high school. We would drink and get high every weekend; I was always the only girl there and would freely black out and pass out as I wished.

I embarrassed myself and my friends time and time again.

I was grounded time and time again, always resolving to drink less, to do better.

I never did.

I didn't know I couldn't.

I justified my drug use in high school by never having my own stash and never smoking alone, but I was adamant about buying my own pipe and my own supply of weed. I didn't just buy a cheap bag—I decided to buy a half ounce of marijuana. I drop to a place where my family was vacationing, with a few cases of beer, a handle of vodka, and a half ounce—fifteen grams—of marijuana in my car. If pulled over, I could have faced thirty days in prison, a fine of $500, or both.

I was putting myself in increasingly dangerous situations for drugs and alcohol.

Yet those thoughts only crossed my mind after the fact.

I was dumped by my long time on-again, off-again high school boyfriend. The breakup was the end of the world. I made a plan to go to a party, find a comfortable chair, and drink to my heart's content.

I started to pregame while I got ready for the night.

I finished an entire bottle of wine.

And another.

An hour later, I stumbled into the party, already blacked out.

Nobody knew. I was a master at covering it up. How could they have known?

That night would change my life.

* * *

I woke up the next morning hurting.

I had bruises on my body and assumed I had fallen, which was common for someone who drank like me.

The bruises and the pain weren't from a fall.

That night I had been raped.

* * *

The next morning, I started to hear what had actually transpired the night before.

I'd stumbled off with two boys.

They would proceed to rape me.

That wasn't how others saw it.

- I'd been drunk.

- I'd put *them* in a terrible position.

- It was wrong of *me* to blame those boys for what I did when I was drunk.

- I was overreacting.

These refrains were told to me over and over as I processed what had happened. When you are told something time and time again, that becomes your truth. My brain eventually blocked that night from my memory, protecting me from the trauma, protecting me from memories of the rape.

It was just the beginning.

INTRODUCTION

———

The United States of America is in the middle of a public health epidemic.

Alcoholism and addiction have endured for centuries in this country; however, in 2019 Americans are dying at startling rates due to their addiction to drugs and alcohol.

The problem is we've created a message that insulates America's colleges and universities from the epidemic.

"It's not alcoholism...until you graduate."

"Alcohol helps you find yourself and lose your inhibitions."

"It's a phase."

"Do it now and get it out of your system."

Unfortunately, we've created a culture that breeds addiction:

- *Prevalence of Drinking:* According to the 2015 NSDUH, 58.0 percent of full-time college students ages eighteen to twenty-two drank alcohol in the past month, compared with 48.2 percent of other persons of the same age.

- *Prevalence of Binge Drinking:* According to the 2015 NSDUH, 37.9 percent of college students ages eighteen to twenty-two reported binge drinking in the past month, compared with 32.6 percent of other persons of the same age.

- *Prevalence of Heavy Alcohol Use:* According to the 2015 NSDUH, 12.5 percent of college students ages eighteen to twenty-two reported heavy alcohol use in the past month compared with 8.5 percent of other persons of the same age. [1]

I started drinking in high school—and it always felt abnormal. When I got to college, suddenly the behaviors that had been frowned around were encouraged and celebrated.

---

[1] Bose, J., Hedden, S. L., Lipari, R. N., & Park-Lee, E. (n.d.). *Key Substance Use and Mental Health Indicators in the United States: Results from the 2015 National Survey on Drug Use and Health*. Retrieved from SAMHSA website: https://www.samhsa.gov/data/sites/default/files/NSDUH-FFR1-2015/NSDUH-FFR1-2015/NSDUH-FFR1-2015.pdf

I'd found the place that would accelerate what I'd started.

I wrote this book for people like me: for those suffering or who have suffered through addiction, for those whose loved ones have met with irreversible consequences, or for those who seek to understand the truth behind addiction and what it entails.

* * *

I started my freshman year of college without a care in the world. I continued to drink abnormally. My first night out, my friends and I attended a "dry party," as it was pledge week for the fraternities in downtown Boston.

Dry? I never went to a dry party.

I pregamed to prepare.

I would drink a half handle of vodka before arriving at the party.

This type of drinking continued every weekend, and though I knew the rest of my friends didn't drink the way I did, I justified it by saying, "they must not have really drank in high school."

While I'd spent the entire summer of getting drunk and high every night, I quit smoking weed due to the prospect of getting drug tested by my NCAA regulated athletics team.

That wouldn't last long.

By mid-October, I broke my thumb. I had reconstructive surgery, as my bone had fractured into three pieces. My mother and father told the doctor not to give me opioid painkillers, as they did when I had my wisdom teeth removed, because they were aware of their addictive qualities.

I was originally prescribed Oxycontin, but due to its wide news coverage of addiction, my parents asked for something else. I was given Tramadol, an opioid painkiller, marketed as a nonaddictive cousin to its stronger counterparts, such as Oxycontin and Percocet. I remember taking them for the first time, my arm in a sling, laying in bed and thinking to myself "I missed being high."

My parents begged me to get rid of them after a couple days, as we had a family member who had graduated from Percocet to heroin a few years earlier. Annoyed with their constant nagging and slightly scared by how much I enjoyed the drugs, I turned them in to health services.

It didn't take long for me to return to chasing the high I loved so much. I had surgery on October 12, 2017.

By Halloween, I was back to smoking weed.

At first it was light smoking with friends, and I didn't have my own supply.

By early November, I had ordered a new pipe and grinder on Amazon and had it shipped to my college mailbox. I then proceeded to go on a month long bender, smoking every single day.

This habit only worsened when the horrors of that night in August, flashbacks of my rapes, came back just before Thanksgiving. The pain I felt—the shame, the dirtiness, the guilt, and the self-hatred—were so unbearable that I could not survive awake or sober.

I lived my life either asleep or high.

I ceased going to classes.

I did not eat.

I barely left my room.

Like clockwork, I went out every night around 9 p.m. to smoke, alone.

It was like I was on autopilot. My hands packed and lit my pipe automatically, without thought. My body thought I needed it to survive.

I remember telling my cousin, "I'm not addicted to weed, I'm emotionally dependent on it."

I was addicted through and through.

* * *

My nights began to look more and more the same.

I'd find some place to be that night where other college students would be drinking.

And then, my routine was the same.

Pregame. Then join the rest of the college students who were "just like me," or so I told myself.

* * *

This book will not succeed in encompassing the entirety of this crisis, but my hope is that it will identify the barriers in this country that inhibit Americans from addressing and surviving alcoholism and addiction.

This book shares my story—as a narrative to take you through the dark and scary path I was on—and how college has created a culture that celebrates drugs and alcohol in a way that is no longer "just what you do."

My hope is you'll see a different picture than what is glorified in movies and television.

My hope is to facilitate a conversation.

* * *

As my first semester drew to a close, suicidal thoughts started to creep in.

Passing cars seemed to me like fleeting opportunities, and the immense amount of antidepressants I had looked like a good option to down in one swallow. I remember looking for the Tramadol in my psychosis, but it was gone, thank God.

In early December, I found myself on the roof of a college building, toeing the ledge.

I was contemplating jumping.

I experienced an angel and a devil—one telling me I would never escape the pain, the other telling me that it was not my time.

I felt a hand on my shoulder gently pull me back. There was no one on the roof with me. I was alone.

This moment was my first spiritual experience; something told me, *"Get off the roof."*

* * *

The next few days were a blur.

I was taken to the counseling center, where I was told I needed to be hospitalized. I talked myself out of that pretty quickly and tried to convince the people trying to help me that I was okay.

When I came back to my dorm, I told my roommate I wanted to die. I'll never forget the words that came out of her mouth, as they very well might have saved me: "Maggie, if you kill yourself, it will ruin my life."

It wasn›t about me anymore, it was about her.

She didn't let me smoke alone that night.

We burned the clothes I was raped in and I haven't put a drug or a drink into my body since.

December 5.

I called my high school psychologist from all those years ago, who now lived in California and hadn't seen me since my junior year of high school. I told her everything and she convinced me to go home.

The next day, I called my mom.

She dropped everything to drive six hours from Philadelphia to pick me up. That day, my roommate and I tied up all my loose ends in order to be issued a cease and release, meaning I would not be finishing my first semester of college.

That night, in a hotel, in my mother's care, the withdrawal started. The sweats, shakes, and immense craving were horrible, but I knew I couldn't go back.

I went home to Philadelphia and was given the option to go to rehab, a psychiatric hospital, or attend outpatient therapy. I chose the latter, in hopes that it would be the easiest. However, I couldn't get into a program—they were full and had monthslong waits.

Nevertheless, I was still scared I would kill myself, so I attended my first twelve-step meeting on December 7.

The rest is history.

My sobriety date is December 5, 2017.

I work a twelve-step program with a sponsor. I sponsor others. I have never been more grateful to be alive.

Sobriety is hard work and a labor of love. I am a different person than I was the last time I got high or drunk. I know now that I suffer from a disease called alcoholism, a fatal disease that tried, and failed, to kill me. Every day I fight a battle to stay sober, but it is worth it, because without the efforts I have put in, I would not be alive today. I have peace, self-love, and faith. I do not wish to die, nor do I wish to use drugs and alcohol to block my emotional pain and trauma. Despite my depression, anxiety, and PTSD, I do not drink or use drugs.

I don't have to live that way anymore.

I was eighteen years old when I got clean and sober.

I am grateful for the life I have today.

CHAPTER ONE

OUR TRAUMATIZED GENERATION

———

As I walk through any airport, my head is on a constant swivel.

I survey the area, trying to identify possible threats.

A tall man looks up and makes eye contact with me in Starbucks; one briskly walks past me, probably late for his flight, but alerts my brain to potential danger.

At night I used to wake up in a cold sweat, panicked and afraid. Night terrors simulated the trauma I had suffered, now over a year ago. Though now medicated, these nightmares come back when something re-triggers me.

This is what PTSD feels like for me, a sexual assault survivor.

For many others, it looks and feels similar or completely different.

Regardless, it is a horrible, unwanted, inescapable reality that many must face every day.

* * *

Fifty to 66 percent of those who suffer from PTSD also simultaneously battle addiction. [2]

PTSD is a disorder that will affect about seven to eight out of one hundred people in their lifetime, the National Institute of Mental Health (NIMH) reports.[3]

PTSD is brought on by the experience of a traumatic or life-threatening event. This definition includes, but is not limited to, car accidents, sexual assault, childhood trauma, and military service.

---

2   Szalavitz, M. (2012, August 15). How PTSD and Addiction Can Be Safely Treated Together. *Time Magazine*. Retrieved from http://healthland.time.com/2012/08/15/how-ptsd-and-addiction-can-be-safely-treated-together/

3   Post-Traumatic Stress Disorder. (n.d.). Retrieved from National Institute of Mental Health website: https://www.nimh.nih.gov/health/topics/post-traumatic-stress-disorder-ptsd/index.shtml

The Substance Abuse and Mental Health Services Administration (SAMHSA) reported in 2015 that one in fifteen veterans had a substance use disorder in the past year. [4]

Billy Bob Brown Jr., a former US marine and current analyst at the Department of Homeland Security, grew up in Abilene, Texas, in the '70s. Billy's father, Billy Bob Sr., grew up in Marshall. He had been given draft deferrals while in college, but, in 1962, he was going to be drafted into the army, so he went the same day to the Air Force recruiter and volunteered to join.

He went to Vietnam as an Air Force navigator flying AC-130s, suffering from PTSD upon his return to the states.

However, Billy never knew the severity of his symptoms. His mother, a high school librarian, was explicit when it came to teaching her sons about drugs. In high school, he started to recognize that his dad drank to excess. "He had a bottle of Jim Beam or Jack Daniels by his bedside every night." Billy's mother later revealed to him that his father's service as a navigator, flying in combat cargo aircrafts, brought on

4   Bose, J., Hedden, S. L., Lipari, R. N., & Park-Lee, E. (n.d.). *Key Substance Use and Mental Health Indicators in the United States: Results from the 2015 National Survey on Drug Use and Health.* Retrieved from SAMHSA website: https://www.samhsa.gov/data/sites/default/files/NSDUH-FFR1-2015/NSDUH-FFR1-2015/NSDUH-FFR1-2015.pdf

terrible nightmares that would wake him up in the middle of the night, screaming.

Billy's father used alcohol to try to sleep through the night. High levels of stress can make it more likely for a person to turn to drugs or alcohol as a means of escape.

According to American Addiction Centers,

"When someone feels stressed, levels of GABA (gamma-aminobutyric acid) are lowered, and adrenaline is increased. GABA is a kind of natural tranquilizer produced by the brain that can also be stimulated by drugs that suppress the central nervous system, like opioids, marijuana, alcohol, and benzodiazepines. Drugs also increase the presence of dopamine in the brain, one of the brain's chemical messengers that tells a person to feel happy. When the substances wear off, low moods are common as dopamine levels drop."[5]

With continued drug use, the brain struggles to regulate dopamine, adrenaline, and GABA normally; therefore, the

---

5   PTSD and Addiction: The Connection Between Trauma and Drug Addiction. (n.d.). Retrieved from American Addiction Centers website: https://americanaddictioncenters.org/ptsd

brain continues to crave drugs to achieve a high level of dopamine and adrenaline. [6]

* * *

A dual diagnosis of addiction and PTSD is not uncommon.

In fact, studies of inpatient substance abuse treatment centers have found that half of all those receiving treatment for addiction also suffered from simultaneous PTSD.[7]

When my trauma flashbacks were at their worst, I needed drugs to escape.

Now that I am sober, I cannot escape. I must work through my trauma. Behavioral therapy, such as cognitive behavioral therapy (CBT), has helped me learn how to better manage stress, deal with triggers, and mend my self-esteem and negative perceptions of the world around me.

According to Rape, Abuse & Incest National Network (RAINN) 2017 statistics, an American is sexually assaulted every ninety-two seconds. [8]

---

6   Ibid.
7   Ibid.
8   Statistics. (n.d.). Retrieved from Rape, Abuse & Incest National Network website: https://www.rainn.org/statistics

Additionally,

- In the United States, one in five women and one in seventy-one men will be sexually assaulted at some point in their life.

- One in four girls and one in six boys will be sexually abused before they turn eighteen years old.

- One in five women and one in sixteen men are sexually assaulted while in college.[9]

Unsurprisingly, rape is the most under-reported crime, with only 63 percent of sexual assaults being reported to the police and 12 percent of child sexual abuse reported to authorities (NSVRC, 2015).

Those who do not report sexual assault incidents are less likely to receive appropriate treatment, which can lead to months and likely years of struggling with anxiety, depression, intrusive memories, and intimacy difficulties.

---

9 *Statistics About Sexual Violence*. (n.d.). Retrieved from National Sexual Violence Resource Center website: https://www.nsvrc.org/sites/default/files/publications_nsvrc_factsheet_media-packet_statistics-about-sexual-violence_0.pdf

More specifically, NSVRC (2015) research on sexual assault found:

- 33 percent of women who are raped contemplate suicide.

- 13 percent of women who are raped attempt suicide.

- Survivors are 3.4 times more likely to use marijuana than the general public.

- Survivors are six times more likely to use cocaine than the general public.

- Survivors are ten times more likely to use other major drugs than the general public.[10]

* * *

PTSD is not exclusive to survivors of sexual assault.

Post-traumatic stress disorder was a major military problem during World War I, commonly referred to as "shell shock." Furthermore, up to half of military discharges during

---

10 *Statistics About Sexual Violence.* (n.d.). Retrieved from National Sexual Violence Resource Center website: https://www.nsvrc.org/sites/default/files/publications_nsvrc_factsheet_media-packet_statistics-about-sexual-violence_0.pdf

World War II may have been related to post-traumatic stress, according to the National Center for PTSD.

Today, the United States Department of Veterans Affairs, a federal cabinet-level agency, provides near comprehensive health care services to eligible military veterans at VA medical centers and outpatient clinics throughout the country.

According to the VA, the number of veterans with PTSD varies by service era:

- **Operations Iraqi Freedom (OIF) and Enduring Freedom (OEF):** Between 11 and 20 percent out of veterans who served in OIF or OEF have PTSD in a given year.

- **Gulf War (Desert Storm):** About 12 percent of Gulf War veterans have PTSD in a given year.

- **Vietnam War:** About fifteen percent of Vietnam veterans were currently diagnosed with PTSD at the time of the most recent study in the late 1980s, the National Vietnam Veterans Readjustment Study (NVVRS). It is estimated that about 30 percent of Vietnam Veterans have had PTSD in their lifetime.[11]

---

11   How Common is PTSD in Veterans? (n.d.). Retrieved from U.S. Department of Veteran Affairs website: https://www.ptsd.va.gov/understand/common/common_veterans.asp

* * *

PTSD in the military is not limited to veterans. In 1945, Dorothy Still, a nurse in the US Navy, met with a Navy psychiatrist to discuss disturbing symptoms she had been experiencing, as reported by *The New York Times* in May 2019.[12]

Still was one of twelve Navy nurses who had been held prisoner of war by the Japanese military in the occupied Philippines during World War II. For more than three years, Still and the other nurses had provided care to diseased, starving, and destitute civilian inmates in a makeshift infirmary at the POW camp.

She most likely suffered from what today we would call post-traumatic stress disorder, but the Navy psychiatrist offered no support or solutions. Instead, he called her a "fake" and a "liar."[13] Nurses, he claimed, could not suffer the kind of shell shock from war that sailors or soldiers could.

Mental health experts now recognize that PTSD can indeed affect nurses, both military and civilian. As many as 28

---

12   Le Beau Lucchesi, E. (n.d.). For Nurses, Trauma Can Come With the Job. *The New York Times*. Retrieved from https://www.nytimes.com/2019/05/07/well/live/for-nurses-trauma-can-come-with-the-job.html

13   Ibid.

percent of nurses experience PTSD at some point in their careers, said Meredith Mealer, an associate professor at the Anschutz Medical Campus at the University of Colorado, Denver, though health care providers still often struggle to treat it.[14]

The stressful environment of nursing can support many of the "triggers and traumas of PTSD," Mealer said. "Nurses see people die. They work on resuscitating patients. They try to control bleeding. They have end-of-life discussions. And sometimes they are verbally or physically abused by patients or visiting family members."[15]

* * *

In the United States, the percentage of nurses with PTSD is equivalent to the percent of people who have witnessed a mass shooting—28 percent, according to the National Center for PTSD.[16]

Since 1966, 1,102 Americans have been killed in mass shootings, according to an analysis by *The Washington*

---

14 Ibid.
15 Ibid.
16 Novotney, A. (n.d.). What happens to the survivors. *The American Psychological Association*. Retrieved from https://www.apa.org/monitor/2018/09/survivors

Post.[17] Thousands more have been injured—both physically and psychologically.

In April of 1999, thirteen high school students were murdered in Littleton, Colorado, in the Columbine High School Shooting. In May of 1999, I was born.

Since then, there have been fifty mass shootings involving the death of five or more people, in the United States. The shootings at Virginia Tech, Tucson, Aurora, Sandy Hook, Charleston, San Bernardino, Pulse Nightclub, Las Vegas, and Marjory Stoneman Douglas High School all captured the nation's attention; however, the US government has yet to enact comprehensive gun reform.

Educators in a post-Columbine era have a unique and profound challenge: how to prepare young students for an active shooter in their classroom, without provoking anxiety or fear.

In Akron, Ohio, safety days are used to teach young students how to stack chairs and desks to make it hard for "bad guys" to get in. In other schools, "Mr. Lock" is asked to come to the office over the loudspeaker, signaling to teachers to get

17   Ibid.

into a "safe area," bar the door and instruct students to hide in silence.[18]

This training has been proven so upsetting and traumatizing to some children, and even parents, that euphemisms have been implemented, especially in young classrooms: a bear or escaped zoo animals running loose in the school, for example.

Children start to see through these stories, creating distrust between students and teachers. One fifth grader worried how she'll know if the drill is real or not. Children as young as two years old practice "self-control" drills, which involve their teachers instructing them to learn how to sit quietly in a lockdown.

A growing number of school districts are shifting from lockdown drills and hiding in classrooms to multi-option response drills, which ideally end with an escape. These multi-option drills can consist of instructing children to run in a zigzag pattern, throwing objects or screaming to distract the shooter. Protocol ALICE (alert, lockdown, inform, counter, evacuate) was the standard for most active

18 Blad, E. (2017). Do Schools' 'Active-Shooter' Drills Prepare or Frighten? *Education Week*. Retrieved from https://www.edweek.org/ew/articles/2017/09/20/do-schools-active-shooter-drills-prepare-or-frighten.html

shooter drills, but ALICE made teachers and parents uneasy, knowing their children were sitting ducks.[19]

As reported in *The Atlantic*, "a generation of Americans came of age hiding under desks from nuclear bombs."[20] Some teachers saw a clear psychological difference in their students. Evidence could be found in children's artwork—mushroom clouds and planes circling above were not uncommon. Following the shooting at Sandy Hook Elementary in Connecticut, twenty states passed specific laws requiring drills in public schools.

Across the country, educators, parents, and law enforcement officers are looking for solutions. The ALERRT (Advanced Law Enforcement Rapid Response Training) facility founded at Texas State University has become the federal standard for active shooter training. Founded in 2002, these training facilities, complete with full-sized schools, are used to play out active shooter scenarios. Officers are even trained to act as temporary medics to ensure victims don't bleed out before SWAT teams and EMTs can arrive at the scene.

---

19 Ibid.
20 Hamblin, J. (2018). What Are Active-Shooter Drills Doing to Kids? *The Atlantic*. Retrieved from https://www.theatlantic.com/health/archive/2018/02/effects-of-active-shooter/554150/

Preparedness can be a good thing, but as children are forming their perceptions of the world, knowing they can be shot in what should be a safe environment is dangerous. I personally feel my perception of school was altered due to these seemingly high-risk drills. Though we were reassured the drills were not real, the fear of when the drills would become real became a constant in my mind. The psychological effect of mass shootings is apparent among American students across the country. Mass shootings are mentally distressing to students, especially due to the persistent media coverage each school shooting receives.

School should be a positive learning environment, not a fortress. Due to the media coverage of the Parkland shooting, the future of schools may include monitored perimeters, armed guards, and possibly armed teachers, as suggested by President Donald Trump, instead of acting as safe havens for American children. Schools are becoming more and more like prisons, and "elementary school children are being recruited into a very young army."[21]

The Gabrielle Giffords Law Center to Prevent Gun Violence reports that kids experience psychological harm from

---

21 Leefeldt, E. (2017, November 30). Are active shooter drills too scary for schoolchildren? Retrieved from CBS News website: https://www.cbsnews.com/news/active-shooter-drills-lockdowns-too-scary-for-schoolchildren/

shootings even if they have not been exposed to gun violence, and 60 percent of high school students who have not been exposed to gun violence say they fear it—that's just students who haven't experienced gun violence! Forty percent of students who have been exposed to gun violence have PTSD.[22] Gun violence is a disease that has infected the youngest minds in our country. Students who live in communities with a higher rate of gun violence are more at risk for emotional distress. Drills and training may be well-intentioned, but they exacerbate underlying fears of gun violence.

Children are growing up in a time of uncertainty, never knowing what is going to happen. Losing the feeling of safety, especially at school, at an early age has a significant impact on a child's development

Tackling and talking about these issues at home can be difficult, as reported in *USA Today*, and children know when something is wrong. Dad comforting Mom, Mom crying at the TV, or parents acting reluctant to drop them off at school are all indicators to children.

---

22 *Protecting the Next Generation*. (2016, March). Retrieved from Giffords Law Center to Prevent Gun Violence website: https://lawcenter. giffords.org/protecting-next-generation/

Though measures such as guards, multi-option response drills instead of lock-downs, and other changes at school may aim to create a feeling of security, children will react differently in this age of school shootings. The National Child Traumatic Stress Network (NCTSN) warns that following any mass shooting, children may experience "sadness, grief, hopelessness, anxiety, and anger."[23] The NCTSN urges parents to start the conversation; however, *USA Today* and NBC advise parents to talk to their children at an "age appropriate level." Children younger than five are normally too young to understand the impact of a mass shooting; however, older children or siblings may tell their younger counterparts about guns, shootings, and other school violence.

NBC's "Today" show reports that when children are "old enough to ask, they are old enough to know." Jennifer Hartstein, a child psychologist and guest on *Today*, advises parents to let their children take the lead and be careful not to give too much information.

According to *USA Today*, parents of preschoolers should limit their child's exposure to social media and the news and censor

---

23   The National Child Traumatic Stress Network. (2014). *Talking to Children about the Shooting* [Pamphlet]. Retrieved from https://www.nctsn.org/sites/default/files/resources//talking_to_children_about_the_shooting.pdf

their own conversation in the household. Children watch their parents very closely, so it is important for them to be mindful of their own reactions to these tragedies. Elementary school children should be asked about their knowledge of the incident. Parents should encourage their children to ask them questions and respond with direct answers.

Parents of middle and high school age kids should be asked directly about their feelings and be given the facts, which includes correcting inaccurate information. When talking to children about mass shootings, the NCTSN advises limiting media, being a positive role model, and seeking extra help, such as therapy, if a child is particularly distressed following a shooting.

With schools continuing to move toward aggressive, rather than passive, responses to active shooter drills, parents should be able to provide the necessary support their children need at home. However, not all children belong to a family or household where emotional support is common; therefore, teachers should also engage in open dialogue with their students.

* * *

I grew up scared, locked in a janitor's closet, waiting for "Mr. Lock" to leave my elementary school. As I got older, the drills were sparse, but the seed of danger at school was planted in my head at an early age.

Through middle school, the news was flooded with mass shooting coverage, and, as I got into high school, excited about the prospect of college, I saw campuses seeing the same violence too. The threat was ever present, and I spent years in therapy talking about my fears of being attacked at school. In the city of Philadelphia alone, we saw more gun violence on the news every day than we did weather reports.

Gun violence is a disease that has spread throughout this nation, I've known from an early age that nowhere is safe, even at school.

Mass shootings and police brutality have dominated the news cycle for years. Today, live streaming, Tweets, and Facebook posts have blasted the incidents of police brutality into the mainstream media.

For many black youth, the disproportionate and often traumatic experience of police arrest and use of force against them, their family members and friends, the combination of race and authority is often lethal.

Many of us will never forget the name, Trayvon Martin, a seventeen-year-old who was followed, shot, and killed by neighborhood watchman George Zimmerman in Sanford, Florida, in 2012.

President Barack Obama captured the nation when he decided to weigh in, despite being famously reluctant to speak to the country on issues of race. "You know, if I had a son, he'd look like Trayvon ..." The president later stated, "Another way of saying that is: Trayvon Martin could have been me 35 years ago."[24]

Obama surprised reporters by delivering deeply personal remarks after Zimmerman was acquitted. "There are very few African American men in this country who haven't had the experience of being followed when they were shopping in a department store. That includes me," he said.[25]

"There are very few African American men who haven›t had the experience of walking across the street and hearing the locks click on the doors of cars. That happened to me—at least before I was a senator."[26]

---

24 The White House, Office of the Press Secretary. (2013, July 19). *Remarks by the President on Trayvon Martin*[Press release]. Retrieved from https://obamawhitehouse.archives.gov/the-press-office/2013/07/19/remarks-president-trayvon-martin
25 Ibid.
26 Ibid.

In America, violent crime rates are down significantly since 1993, when the nation's gun homicide rate hit its peak. Rhere are still neighborhoods in cities like Oakland, Detroit, New Orleans, and Newark, New Jersey, where shootings are a constant occurrence and where the per capita murder rates are drastically higher than in the rest of the country.

Some 3,500 American troops were killed during the eight-year war in Iraq. Within the same time period, 3,113 people were killed on the streets of Philadelphia. According to FBI data, between 2002 and 2012 Chicago lost more than five thousand people to homicide—that's nearly three times the number of Americans killed in action in Afghanistan.[27]

Over the past twenty years, medical researchers have found new ways to quantify the effects of the relentless violence on America's inner cities. They surveyed residents who had been exposed to violence in cities such as Detroit and Baltimore and noticed symptoms of PTSD: nightmares, obsessive thoughts, and a constant sense of danger.

In a series of federally funded studies in Atlanta, researchers interviewed more than eight thousand inner

---

27 Beckett, L. (2014, September 5). The Hidden Cost of Gun Violence: Meet a Mother and Her 7-Year-Old With PTSD. Retrieved from ProPublica website: https://www.propublica.org/article/meet-a-mother-and-her-seven-year-old-with-ptsd

city residents, most of them African American. Two thirds of respondents said they had been violently attacked at some point in their lives. Half knew someone who had been murdered. Of the women interviewed, a third had been sexually assaulted.[28]

Roughly 30 percent of respondents had symptoms consistent with PTSD—a rate as high or higher than that of veterans of the Vietnam, Iraq, or Afghanistan wars.[29]

* * *

PTSD affects 8 percent of Americans, equivalent to the population of the state of Texas.[30] Millions must learn to cope with this horrifying and unwanted illness. In a nation witnessing and experiencing trauma, drugs and alcohol are easy solutions to escape.

I found relief when drunk and high, but this solution had an expiration date.

Weed isn't a gateway drug. Alcohol isn't a gateway drug.

---

28 Ibid.
29 Ibid.
30 How Common is PTSD in Adults? (n.d.). Retrieved from U.S. Department of Veteran Affairs website:https://www.ptsd.va.gov/ understand/common/common_adults.asp

Trauma is the gateway. Child abuse is the gateway. Neglect is the gateway. Rape is the gateway.

Drug and alcohol abuse are the symptoms, not the causes, of bigger issues.

CHAPTER TWO

THE DISEASE DOES NOT DISCRIMINATE

———

In early sobriety, still less than six months, I began to explore the Internet to learn more about addiction.

I stumbled upon a 2016 MTV documentary, starring American rapper Macklemore. Macklemore, given name Ben Haggerty, was addicted to Oxycontin and Percocet for many years, first introduced to him through his mother's medicine cabinet. Though he first got sober in 2008, attending treatment with financial help from his parents, Macklemore admits he has relapsed since then, describing addiction as an "ongoing battle" and a "lifelong disease."[31]

---

31 MTV. (2016, October 11). *Prescription for Change: Ending America's Opioid Crisis*[Video file]. Retrieved from https://www.youtube.com/watch?v=2QePuumO310

A celebrity such as Macklemore opening up about his addiction and sobriety was important for someone like me. As a college student clinging desperately to her life and her sobriety, hearing other people›s stories, famous or not, was essential. Not only did the documentary bring me comfort in those early months of sobriety, it also provided me an education about the disease I was suffering from and ultimately led to my personal research.

* * *

The opioid epidemic is the worst addiction crisis in US history, with two million opioid addicts around the country. Drug overdoses have skyrocketed, with prescription opioids accounting for 44 percent of all drug overdose deaths, followed by heroin, benzodiazepines, such as Valium and Xanax, and cocaine.[32]

In an interview with Macklemore and President Obama, Obama stated that the United States must "treat [addiction] not as a moral failing, but as a public health problem that can be solved."[33]

Addiction has continued to prevail throughout the United States, but prescription opioids are a relatively new poison

---

32 Ibid.
33 Ibid.

entering the conversation. In 1996, Purdue Pharma introduced a "wonder drug" called Oxycontin. The pharmaceutical company spend hundreds of millions of dollars to convince doctors that their product was safe and nonaddictive. As sales rose, so did overdose deaths. As patients built up a tolerance to the pills, they moved on to heroin.[34]

Over twenty years later, the opioid epidemic has grown to a national emergency.

To understand prescription opioids, it is important to understand how they affect the brain of an addict.

* * *

The human body produces natural opioids for when you are injured, such as a sprained ankle or toothache. These natural opioids attach to receptors in your brain. Prescription opioids are used to alleviate immense pain, such as after a major surgery. The downside to these painkillers is that they also produce dopamine, a chemical that helps the brain recognize what it needs for survival, such as food, water, or air. Heavy use of the pills leads to training the brain to think it needs the drugs to survive.

---

34   MTV. (2016, October 11). *Prescription for Change: Ending America's Opioid Crisis*[Video file]. Retrieved from https://www.youtube.com/watch?v=2QePuumO310

An addict in recovery can retrain their brain the longer they are without the substance in their system. "For so many people around the country, when they›re ready to try [treatment], they've got to wait 3 months, 6 months, a year, to get into a facility," Obama says to Macklemore. "We've got to create an environment that when folks are ready, [treatment] is there and if you don't succeed the first time, that there›s follow up. This is especially true in under-served communities, rural communities," Obama continues.[35]

Addiction is treatable and recovery is possible.

However, one size does not fit all.

* * *

Medications, such as Vivitrol, Suboxone, and Methadone, can be helpful. Most need treatment for other conditions, whether they be physical or psychological. Treatment must be long term and works best when it is available at the time addicts are ready.

My friend, Alice, has been aided by a maintenance drug treatment program. "For me it›s been the best decision that I've made."

---

35 Ibid.

Maintenance drug treatment programs are commonly used to treat addiction to opioids. However, because maintenance drugs are themselves opioids, few have been willing to accept such programs, believing they replace one addiction with another.

This belief has kept many addicts from receiving the treatment they need. In fact, many treatment facilities, that were otherwise evidence-based, did not allow patients to use these medications, in favor of an "abstinence only" philosophy.

Drugs such as Suboxone, Vivitrol, and Methadone are commonly used in maintenance drug treatment programs. Methadone is the most widely used, replacing the opioids in an addict's system with milder effects. The goal is to aid addicts as they withdraw from stronger substances such as heroin or Oxycontin. However, Methadone has been handicapped by restrictive government regulations and prejudice against maintenance drugs in general.

Vivitrol is another drug commonly used to treat addiction. It is an extended-release treatment medication administered once a month via an intramuscular injection. The difficulty with Vivitrol is that patients must detox and remain abstinent from their drug of choice, commonly heroin, for seven to ten days prior to starting Vivitrol. Otherwise, patients can be sent into extreme withdrawal symptoms. Many addicts cannot withstand the seven to ten day period of withdrawal. Therefore, they many relapse or die before being administered Vivitrol.

However, for those who maintain their sobriety, Vivitrol can lead them to long-term recovery.

Suboxone, another drug used to treat withdrawal, is a combination of buprenorphine and Naloxone, an opioid antagonist commonly known as Narcan. Naloxone blocks opioid receptors, which prevents the body from experiencing the opioid effects of buprenorphine. This combination was designed to discourage users from abusing Suboxone, since they cannot achieve a high from the drug.

Though thousands of addicts achieve recovery with the assistance of maintenance drug treatment, for some, these programs can be harmful. Patients who take drugs such as Methadone or Suboxone can stay on their treatment programs for many years. However, if they become unable to afford their medication or need to stop their treatment, withdrawing from the medication can lead to relapse.

The ultimate goal is to wean off the medication, but doctors should be careful to taper the medication gradually, which may take months or years. Similarly to a broken arm that has been in a cast for an extended period of time, the brain must recover from long-term drug use, benefiting from external supports in the form of medication. In cases of serious and long-term opioid use disorder, a patient may need these supports indefinitely.

Alice wanted to do her Suboxone program the right way, with counseling and monitoring. "I didn't want to just go to a Suboxone doctor, have them write me a script for 30 days...I still needed someone to be accountable to."

* * *

Sadly, only one in ten addicts will get the treatment they need due to roadblocks such as waiting time, insurance, and poverty.

In addition, few programs implement up-to-date science.

There is progress being made in regard to these issues. The number of people in the United States without insurance has begun to decline and treatment centers are starting to catch up scientifically. Advocates need to continue to fight until everyone with an addiction has immediate access to quality, affordable care without shame or barriers.

Most treatment programs last twenty-eight to thirty days, as the brain only starts healing after thirty days. "The tragedy of how we've been dealing with the war on drugs generally over the last thirty years is that we haven't emphasized treatment, recovery, treated it as a public health problem, but have so often thought of this just as a criminal law problem and a throw folks in jail problem," Obama admits. "The good news is that awareness is starting to rise, and I'll be honest with you, part of what's starting the change is that the opioid crisis is getting into communities that are suburban, relatively well-to-do, rural communities, white communities, and people's kids who are being affected, are folks who have a voice and they're starting to recognize that generally how we've dealt with reduction of addiction and drugs has been often times counterproductive and we need to shift a lot more resources into treatment. But we're still way short of where we need to be."[36]

Obama is correct: addiction is treated as a criminal justice issue in this country, but why? In the '80s, crack cocaine flooded predominantly black communities. Therefore, in 2001, 45 percent of Americans supported tough drug laws, partly because racial bias.[37]

However, in 2016, the Center for Disease Control and Prevention (CDC) reported that per one hundred thousand

---

36 MTV. (2016, October 11). *Prescription for Change: Ending America's Opioid Crisis*[Video file]. Retrieved from https://www.youtube.com/watch?v=2QePuumO310

37 Ibid.

opioid deaths, 8.4 were Native Americans, followed by 7.9 white victims and 3.3 black victims.[38]

When white people are suffering from addiction, Americans are more likely to see it as a disease instead of a crime.

Given the shift in demographics toward a largely affected white population, 67 percent of Americans support treatment over punishment. Federal spending has begun to move away from law enforcement and into treatment.[39]

Obama points to the medical community for making pharmaceutical treatment the most inexpensive solution post-op for patients rather than physical therapy. The United States needs to educate future doctors and nurses. With 260 million opioid prescriptions prescribed per year, every adult American could have a bottle of pills for themselves.[40]

Physicians have faced their own roadblocks. Doctors are unaware of a patient's drug abuse history and often don't know whether an addict already has a prescription. Physicians have created a solution: an online database to cross reference to see if an addict already has been prescribed opioids.

---

38 Ibid.
39 MTV. (2016, October 11). *Prescription for Change: Ending America's Opioid Crisis*[Video file]. Retrieved from https://www.youtube.com/watch?v=2QePuumO310
40 Ibid.

Due to solutions such as this screening and new federal guidelines, opioid prescriptions are declining in the United States

Americans need to understand that you do not need opioid painkillers for a sprained ankle, broken arm, or wisdom tooth recovery.

We need Big Pharma to be honest about their products and doctors to prescribe opiates only when they're absolutely necessary. We need to think of addiction as a treatable medical condition so people can openly ask for help like they would for any illness. We need to improve treatment so that it's scientific and long-term. We need to shift money away from incarceration and into accessible treatment.

* * *

The MTV documentary follows multiple addicts in recovery in Macklemore's hometown of Seattle, Washington.

Lindsay was prescribed Vicodin when she suffered a neck injury at twelve years old. After Vicodin, she discovered Oxycontin and, eventually, heroin. She lost everything to heroin in a matter of four months: her job and custody of her children. Lindsay has dedicated her life to addicts like herself.

She started the nonprofit Hope Soldiers, which helps addicts with no money or insurance get into treatment.

"It's really important that addicts know they're not alone," Lindsay says, "that they are a person worthy of love, honor, dignity and respect."

Following Lindsay through Seattle we see her giving out food and her phone number to people addicted, living in a makeshift camp in the woods. We also see her helping her friend Alaina, who wants to detox from heroin. Alaina has an appointment with a Suboxone doctor. She must be in withdrawal for the treatment to succeed. However, Alaina secretly uses heroin the morning of her appointment, followed by an opioid blocker to reverse the effects of the heroin. The blocker instead sends her into immediate and severe withdrawal. Within thirty minutes, Alaina is violently sick. Lindsay is called and she carries Alaina out of the house, taking her to the emergency room.

On the ride there, Lindsay cradles an almost lifeless Alaina. "She doesn't want to be like this," Lindsay says, "she's just trapped right now."

Returning home after six hours in the emergency room, Alaina resigns to her bed to recover. "I've yelled, I've cried, I've pleaded and I've begged," Alaina's mom tells Lindsay. "None of it matters...I'll probably end up burying my daughter." This reality is one many parents have to face when they have a child struggling with addiction.

* * *

Macklemore is not the only famous musician who has opened up about his recovery from drugs and alcohol. Demi Lovato, a child star turned pop icon, has been very open about her mental health and recovery.

In her 2017 documentary *Simply Complicated*, fans are able to see Demi facing her demons while simultaneously recording her album, *Tell Me You Love Me*.[41]

Demi describes herself as always being an "outcast." After being bullied in elementary school, Demi began to "party" at a young age. She was seventeen years old, working forDisney Channel, when she first tried cocaine. She remembers already feeling out of control that first time.

Demi's father, Patrick, was an alcoholic and an addict.

---

41 *Demi Lovato: Simply Complicated - Official Documentary*[Video file]. (2017, October 17). Retrieved from https://www.youtube.com/watch?v=ZWTlL_w8cRA

"I always searched for what he found in drugs and alcohol," Demi shared, "because it fulfilled him and he chose that over a family."[42]

Demi's parents ultimately divorced; her mother remarried and her father died of cancer in 2013. As Demi reflects upon her childhood, she recounts experiencing depression from a young age. Nevertheless, she and her sister participated in beauty pageants in their home state of Texas and took up modeling. It wasn't long until Demi fell in love with singing.

The Lovato family committed themselves to Demi's dream and began to go to countless auditions. She booked a role on *Barney & Friends* when she was just seven years old. She didn't realize that once she got that first job, she would put pressure on herself to get the next, desperate to succeed. She would get small roles in pilots of TV shows and finally booked a role on the Disney show *As The Bell Rings*. She learned to play guitar at age eight and learned that song writing could be an outlet for her feelings.

Demi Lovato's big break came at age fifteen old when she got the leading role in a Disney Channel original movie *Camp Rock*. Starring alongside the Jonas Brothers, Demi was signed

---

42 Ibid.

to their manager and immediately went on tour with the Jo Bros, simultaneously recording and making her first album.

Things started moving at a rapid pace.

"Looking back," Demi says, "I think it was a lot for anyone, let alone a kid."[43]

Now doing music, movies, and TV all at the same time, Demi started living a double life. She was squeaky clean for Disney Channel, but once the cameras were off, Demi's dark side came out. Demi's team wanted to blame the star's behavior on the fact she was just a teenage girl, but they soon realized there was a bigger issue.

Demi had anger issues and could easily out manipulate any adult. This behavior came to a breaking point after a party during the *Camp Rock 2: The Final Jam* tour. Demi's team found out she was using Adderall—someone had told Kevin Jonas Sr. Demi recounts manipulating Jonas into telling her who had ratted her out. When she heard it was one of her backup dancers, Demi remembers thinking, "I'm about to beat this b---h up," and she did.[44] That day, Demi boarded

43 *Demi Lovato: Simply Complicated - Official Documentary*[Video file]. (2017, October 17). Retrieved from https://www.youtube.com/watch?v=ZWTlL_w8cRA

44 Ibid.

the plane, and when she reached her backup dancer, she punched her in the face, then continued to sit in her seat and put her hoodie up.

This incident led to her being admitted into treatment for the first time. She was eighteen.

When she was diagnosed with bipolar disorder, Demi says "It just made sense...it wasn't my fault, there was something off with me."[45]

However, Demi relapsed, recalling that she wasn't working her program. "I wasn't ready to get sober."[46] No one knew of her relapse, and she managed to stay out on a two month bender, while actively promoting recovery on air, high.

Demi was eventually introduced to Mike Bayer, founder of CAST Centers addiction and mental health facility in West Hollywood.

"Demi was on a path to suicide," Bayer recounts. "She'd have like bags of pills and an eight ball of coke."[47]

---

45   Ibid.

46   *Demi Lovato: Simply Complicated - Official Documentary*[Video file]. (2017, October 17). Retrieved from https://www.youtube.com/watch?v=ZWTlL_w8cRA

47   Ibid.

Demi went through twenty sober companions while working with Coach Mike. "I was either craving drugs or on drugs," Demi admitted. After attempting to commit suicide, Demi was committed into a psychiatric ward, but it was not enough to motivate the nineteen-year-old to get sober. "It's embarrassing to look back at the person I was," Demi says. "I just knew I needed to get high to get through what I was going through."[48]

Demi's team was at their rope's end and threatened to leave. Her manager, agent, attorney, and everyone would leave if she wouldn't get sober. This approach worked for Demi, she even destroyed her cell phone to prove that she was serious. Her manager described that destroyed cell phone as "the beginning of surrender." It was the cell phone that connected her to "the wrong people, drug dealers."[49]

Demi was now nineteen, a judge on reality competition show *The X Factor*, and in her first year of sobriety. She was living in a sober house, where she was responsible for chores and had no cell phone of her own. She had submitted to the process of recovery.

* * *

---

48 Ibid.
49 Ibid.

In 2017, at twenty-five years old, Demi still fought her demons, even six years sober.

She admitted to relapsing when it comes to her eating disorder, bulimia, which she had been vocal about for many years. She says she "feels very ashamed" when she slips up, her feelings of loneliness leading to her relapses. Demi says that food came before the drugs, binging at the age of eight. "Food was medicine," for Demi, filling that void that so many addicts experience.

Demi's recovery from drugs and alcohol had been sustained for six years, thanks to therapy, her twelve-step program, and honesty. Demi shared that exercise became empowering for her in her recovery. "Working out is a form of meditation to me because im not focused on anything in my head."[50]

* * *

When Demi celebrated six years sober, I had just celebrated ninety days of sobriety.

My mom bought me tickets to her concert in Philadelphia as a gift. I messaged her on Instagram the night before the

50 *Demi Lovato: Simply Complicated - Official Documentary*[Video file]. (2017, October 17). Retrieved from https://www.youtube.com/watch?v=ZWTlL_w8cRA

show: "Demi, I know it's a long shot that you see this but I will be at your show tomorrow night in Philly. I am so excited to see you. I am just under 4 months sober and by the grace of God I was saved from ending my own life in December. Your strength in your own sobriety is incredibly inspiring and your album had been my go to on my way to meetings ever since it was released. Thank you for being vocal about your mental health and your addiction - it gives me hope."

She was powerful on that stage. I remember crying through many of her songs, feeling the pain and struggle she had endured, relating to it in my own way. It was an important night for me. To see someone like Demi talk about her recovery in front of thousands of people gave me strength and made me proud of my own journey.

Not three months later, in June, Demi released the single "Sober," revealing she had relapsed. «Mama, I'm so sorry I'm not sober anymore / And Daddy please forgive me for the drinks spilled on the floor / To the ones who never left me / We've been down this road before I'm so sorry, I'm not sober anymore," Demi sang in the ballad.

The next month, it was widely reported that Demi had been hospitalized for an overdose. She had been revived by Narcan and was reported to be "awake and with her family." Fans across the world commiserated over the tragic event, grateful Demi was still alive.

I received many texts when the news broke online; my friends knew how upset I would be. I was upset, but I did what I would do for any of my friends in the program if they relapsed: I reached out. Knowing she would never see it, I still messaged Demi on Instagram: "Hi Demi, I wanted to message you to remind you that relapse is a part of recovery. Don't let anyone tell you about your own journey. Thank you for being a voice for the recovery community. You and your music have inspired me for years...Happiness will find you again, if it hasn't already. I am so proud of you. You are worth so much to this world. Keep coming. xoxo."

Many were shocked when Demi overdosed, but her friends revealed they saw it coming. She had cut out her sober coach, Mike, months before, and had been heavily using. Following her relapse and the release of "Sober," Demi thought she could do things on her own. However, the overdose was a huge wake up call for her.

Demi spent almost two weeks in the hospital, reportedly suffering from nausea and a high fever, likely detoxing and withdrawing from substances. She then checked into rehab for three months, releasing the following statement to her fans: "I now need time to heal and focus on my sobriety and road to recovery. The love you have all shown me will never be forgotten and I look forward to the day where I can say I came out on the other side. I will keep fighting." Following her three months in an extensive inpatient facility, Demi resurfaced on social media, posting a picture of herself at the polls in November.

Since her release from rehab, Demi seems to have been working diligently on her recovery. She is working out, attending therapy and meetings, as well as spending time with her family and supportive friends.

Watching her journey since her overdose has been powerful for me. Relapse is a part of so many recovery journeys and to see defeat and resilience from someone I looked up to, made me realize that this disease really does not care who you are. Whether you are rich and famous, poor and homeless, or somewhere in between, ultimately the disease of addiction seeks to kill you everyday; it is up to you to decide to live or not. Demi taught me that lesson, as have so many others in my program. Recovery is possible for anyone at any time, as long as they are willing to work for it.

Demi, if you ever read this, thank you. I hope you are healthy and happy.

* * *

Standing in front of the White House, President Obama told Macklemore "anybody that's grown up in America has known people who've struggled with [addiction], and may have had some struggles of their own."[51]

The recovery community is all across the nation, all across the world. We must dismantle barriers such as access to treatment and societal shame that keeps addicts from seeking help.

We all know someone struggling; it's time we offer compassion and love instead of judgement and fear.

51 MTV. (2016, October 11). *Prescription for Change: Ending America's Opioid Crisis*[Video file]. Retrieved from https://www.youtube.com/watch?v=2QePuumO310

CHAPTER THREE

MY DRUG DEALER WAS A DOCTOR

Halfway through my first season of collegiate field hockey, I broke my thumb. No big deal—it was just a finger, after all.

I was referred to a well known hand surgeon in the Boston area and made an appointment. The surgeon had previously worked with a teammate of mine, as well as professional athletes on the Celtics and Patriots. I was in good hands, no pun intended.

After taking X-rays of my thumb, the doctor proceeded to tell me the plan. With my mother on speaker phone, I was told three metal pins would be surgically placed in my thumb to repair my shattered bone. The pins would stay in my hand for a few weeks while my finger healed and then they would be taken out in the office. Though pretty straightforward, the course of action described to me felt daunting. I didn't look forward to having metal spikes sticking out of my hand.

A week later, I was taken back to the hospital for surgery. My mother had graciously flown up from Philly to take care of me post-op, as this was my first time going under anesthetics since my wisdom tooth surgery less than six months earlier. We made our way to the hospital where my surgeon met me in the operating room to check in one last time. As we made small talk, I was put under anesthesia. When I woke up, I was disoriented, and my arm was numb. The doctor had put a nerve block on my right arm while the pins were inserted. It felt like someone else's arm was attached to my body.

Returning home to my dorm room, mom set me up in bed with Netflix and explained the strict regimen of pain killers I would have to take over the next few days. Just as she did when I got my wisdom teeth out, my mother instructed my doctors not to give me opioids. She was told they would prescribe me "extra-strength Tylenol." On my medical records, it says I was originally prescribed Oxycontin. I went home from surgery that day with a prescription for Tramadol.

In 1995, Tramadol, a synthetic opioid, was introduced by Johnson & Johnson as a medication that relieved pain just as well as narcotics like Oxycontin, but wasn't addictive.[52] It was marketed as non addictive due to its lack of dependency during clinical trials. However, the trials examined tramadol use by injection, but it is manufactured—and far more potent—in pill form.

Originally, the Drug Enforcement Administration didn't classify Tramadol as a controlled substance, because the FDA believed it had a low potential for abuse. Despite concerns about Tramadol abuse in the years after its release, the FDA repeatedly determined the drug was not being widely abused, and so left it as an unscheduled drug. This mistake made Tramadol easier to obtain and doctors less concerned for abuse, leading to more prescriptions written. Emergency rooms began to report a growing number of overdoses related to Tramadol. In 2013, nearly forty-five million prescriptions for Tramadol were written for patients in the United States, with the number doubling in just five years.

Finally, in 2014, the DEA designated Tramadol to a Schedule IV controlled substance.[53] Many reported their doctors told them the medication they were taking was nonnarcotic, as

52 Patterson, E., MSCP,NCC,LPC. (n.d.). *Tramadol History and Statistics*(A. Lautieri, B.S., Ed.). Retrieved from American Addiction Centers website: https://drugabuse.com/tramadol/history-statistics/
53 Patterson, E., MSCP,NCC,LPC. (n.d.). *Tramadol History and Statistics*(A. Lautieri, B.S., Ed.). Retrieved from American Addiction Centers website: https://drugabuse.com/tramadol/ history-statistics/

my doctor did. Despite its reputation as being a "safe" opioid, it is still an opioid.

I wouldn't consider myself a recovering opioid addict, but for the short time I used Tramadol, I loved it. My use reminded me of my longing for getting high after two months of binge drinking. I was in denial about the effects of the drugs, denying feeling under the influence, though my roommate at the time clearly remembers me intoxicated. I am not naive to the fact that if my use of the medication were prolonged, I would have been susceptible to getting addicted—not only due to the nature of the drug, but because of the disease I am afflicted with.

Luckily, my parents were persistent in advising me to get rid of the drugs a week or so after my surgery. A family member had previously graduated from Percocet to heroin a few years earlier after treating an injury left over from his participating in collegiate athletics. Many student athletes are exposed to opioids during and following their time in college. Injuries are common, but many collegiate athletes are unaware of the risks posed by their medications following surgery. I am one of many college athletes with an opioid story.

* * *

According to an excerpt from the Sport Science Institute's "guide to understanding and supporting student-athlete mental wellness," found on the National Collegiate Athletic Association (NCAA) website, the percentage of student athletes prescribed narcotics for pain medication is higher than the general student body.[54] Though understandable, with injury and pain a part of competitive athletics, the report fails to acknowledge that the use of prescription opioids with or without a prescription can be dangerous.

Whether a college student is prescribed opioids after ACL surgery or tries Percocet at a party, the risk of addiction remains. College students are already susceptible to the college effect, as heavy and frequent alcohol use increases when students arrive on campus. The prevalence of mood-altering substances on campus such as alcohol, marijuana, narcotics, stimulants, depressants, and hallucinogens has been tracked by campus prevention professions for decades.

* * *

Student athletes, compared to other students, report higher rates of "binge drinking," defined as four or more drinks for

---

54 Hainline, B., Bell, L., & Wilfert, M. (n.d.). *Mind, Body and Sport: Substance use and abuse.* Retrieved from NCAA Sport Science Institute website: http://www.ncaa.org/sport-science-institute/mind-body-and-sport-substance-use-and-abuse

women and five or more for men. Alarmingly, one in five male student athletes who use alcohol report drinking ten or more drinks in an outing when they drink.[55]

I'm not surprised by the data reported by the Sport Science Institute. Binge drinking is the only way student athletes drink. There's no time to drink during the weekend. While other students might be able to go out on an occasional weeknight or multiple nights over the weekend, student athletes are subjected to packed schedules, as well as team and NCAA regulations.

Most collegiate programs follow a 24/48 rule, meaning athletes are prohibited from drinking twenty-four hours before a practice and forty-eight hours before a game. During the season, my team and I go to class throughout the day, head to practice and lift in the evening, eat a meal together, then part ways to do our homework and go to bed. We'll have a few games during the week, but most of our games occur on Saturdays. We're busy!

For me, this busy schedule meant the only opportunity to go out and party during the season was Saturday night—one

55 Hainline, B., Bell, L., & Wilfert, M. (n.d.). *Mind, Body and Sport: Substance use and abuse.* Retrieved from NCAA Sport Science Institute website: http://www.ncaa.org/sport-science-institute/mind-body-and-sport-substance-use-and-abuse

night a week. That's it. Can you blame student athletes for overdoing it when their opportunities are limited?

* * *

Almost every story of opioid addiction begins the same way: the individual experienced acute pain either from trauma or surgery, was prescribed opioids by a doctor, and then couldn't quit.

Many report going in for minor surgery and being discharged with sixty tablets of Oxycontin. Patients would experience significant pain the first couple of days after surgery, using the pills as prescribed. After the pain subsided and ibuprofen could get the job done, they'd stop using the opiate. However, patients who discontinued their medication went through withdrawal. They experienced body aches, restlessness, and insomnia. Most will revert back to taking the medication to feel better.

Even after only taking opiates for a few days, patients can withdraw from the medication. If patients continue to treat their withdrawal with the same medication causing their symptoms, they are more likely to get hooked. According to a recent study published in JAMA Surgery, a vast majority of pills taken for nonmedical reasons, like abuse, are obtained from friends or family members. Forty-two percent to

71 percent of prescribed opioids go unused. That leaves thousands of pill bottles in medicine cabinets, waiting for someone to stumble upon.[56]

Multiple government and public health agencies recommend discarding unused opioids. It's unsafe to flush them down the toilet, as they can contaminate our water supply, but most police stations and commercial pharmacies have bins where unused medications can be safely disposed. However, the rate at which opioids are safely disposed is disappointingly low.

We can do more to combat the opioid epidemic.

* * *

The United States is in the middle of a public health crisis. Nationwide, over forty-seven thousand people died from opioid-related causes in 2017, according to the CDC.

To put the current crisis in context, roughly the same number of people died of opioid-related causes in 2016 as died from HIV/AIDS in 1995, at the height of the HIV/AIDS epidemic. In 2016, more Americans died from opioid-related causes

---

56   Bicket, M., Long, J., Pronovost, P., Wu, C., & JAMA Surgery. (2017). *Prescription Opioid Analgesics Commonly Unused After Surgery: A Systematic Review.*Retrieved from U.S. National Library of Medicine National Institutes of Health website: https://www.ncbi.nlm.nih.gov/pubmed/28768328

than from motor vehicle accidents. Driven by the opioid epidemic, more Americans died from drug overdoses in 2016 than who died fighting in the entire Vietnam War

In Massachusetts, the opioid crisis is particularly acute. The opioid-related death rate in the state is more than twice the national average. The opioid crisis has commonly been framed as a problem afflicting the white population. However, more than 80 percent of drug-related deaths in the white, black, and Hispanic communities are opioid related. The crisis—as the data demonstrates—does not discriminate.

The crisis has worsened in Massachusetts due to multiple factors. Fentanyl has become more common in Massachusetts, especially illicit fentanyl. Fentanyl is an opioid that can be prescribed but is often produced and distributed illegally. It has become much more lucrative than heroin, making it popular among street dealers.

Fentanyl is commonly cut with other drugs, making its users unaware that they are taking it. This lack of knowledge is extremely dangerous as fentanyl is fifty times more potent than heroin and one hundred times stronger than morphine. Other synthetic drugs similar to and sometimes stronger than fentanyl, like carfentanil, continue to emerge.

Nationally, fentanyl has become increasingly prevalent, overtaking heroin and opioid painkillers as the most common drug in opioid-related overdose deaths. This spike is ever more pronounced in Massachusetts. The state has the third highest fentanyl-related death rate in the country, second only to New Hampshire and West Virginia.

Opioid-related deaths are not just high in Massachusetts— they are relatively high throughout New England. Five of the six New England states are in the top ten in fentanyl-related death rates, and all six are in the top fifteen. Well prior to the current opioid epidemic, there were established and frequently used drug routes in New England, with Massachusetts as one of the region's primary hubs, which, unfortunately, made Massachusetts more vulnerable to trafficking.

In 2016, there were 47.1 opioid prescriptions per one hundred people in Massachusetts, calling into question the Massachusetts doctors and their role in the crisis. The National Institute of Health awarded the Boston Medical Center (BMC) $89 million in funding to lead a research study with the goal of reducing opioid deaths. The state of Massachusetts has made great progress providing programs such as community education, accelerated access to medication during hospitalization, jail, and detoxification as well as prevention and intervention programs in communities, schools, and doctors' offices. Moving forward, the crisis in Massachusetts, and the nation, will continue to run rampant if policies are not enacted to address the immense loss of American life. We must hold actors like Big Pharma accountable and unite our communities to combat this devastating epidemic.

* * *

On June 11, 2018, the trial court of the Massachusetts Superior Court received a civil action lawsuit between the Commonwealth of Massachusetts and Purdue Pharma.

In the past decade, eleven thousand people in Massachusetts died from opioid-related overdoses and more than one hundred thousand nonfatal overdoses were suffered. The lawsuit filed by the Commonwealth of Massachusetts, brought to the court by Attorney General Maura Healey, accuses Purdue Pharma of creating the opioid epidemic and profiting from it through "a web of illegal deceit."[57] Attorney General Healey has asked the court to end Purdue's "illegal conduct and make Purdue and its executives pay for the harm they inflicted in [Massachusetts]." "Illegal conduct" refers to Purdue's deceiving doctors and patients to use their

---

57 Commonwealth of Massachusetts v. Purdue Pharma L.P. (Superior Court Civil Action). Retrieved from https://www.mass.gov/files/documents/2018/06/12/Purdue%20Complaint%20FILED.pdf

"dangerous drugs," misleading them to take higher doses and to stay on the drugs for longer periods of time.[58]

The suit claims Purdue and its executives led the deception and pocketed millions of dollars in the process. This lawsuit exemplifies how Purdue Pharma's exquisitely executed marketing strategy of their products has led to a mass public health crisis in the United States.

Doctors in America have become formal drug dealers for thousands of patients, some just looking for pain relief. As the death toll of the opioid crisis continues to rise, US states are pushing for Purdue Pharma to take responsibility. Massachusetts was the first to name Purdue Pharma in a lawsuit, but many US states have since followed.

* * *

The defendants involved in the lawsuit are two companies and sixteen individuals "who oversaw and engaged in a deadly, deceptive scheme to sell opioids in Massachusetts."[59] Defendants include Purdue Pharma Inc., Purdue Pharma L.P., and sixteen individuals, namely Richard Sackler and

---

58 Ibid.
59 Ibid.

his family members, who hold seats on the board of Purdue Pharma Inc.

Opioids are highly addictive narcotics, drugs that have claimed too many lives in the state of Massachusetts. It is the opinion of the state that Purdue Pharma is responsible: "Purdue took advantage of addiction to make money."[60] In the past, physicians reserved opioids for those near the end of life and limited them to short-term treatments. However, after Purdue introduced Oxycontin, opioids were more commonly used to treat pain.

Since 2007, Purdue was able to sell more than seventy million doses of opioids in Massachusetts through sales representatives incentivizing doctors to prescribe opioids, publications to dissuade concerns regarding addiction, and marketing their drugs as revolutionary in pain treatment.

This crisis affected "every community" in the Commonwealth of Massachusetts. Opioids were marketed as a "first line" treatment, "the first thing [patients] would take to treat pain."[61] Purdue discouraged and blocked patients from alternative options such as ibuprofen and Tylenol, claiming

---

60 Ibid.
61 Commonwealth of Massachusetts v. Purdue Pharma L.P. (Superior Court Civil Action). Retrieved from https://www.mass.gov/files/documents/2018/06/12/Purdue%20Complaint%20FILED.pdf

"life-threatening side effects," however, maintaining that opioids were "the gold standard of pain medications."[62] Purdue not only explicitly targeted doctors and patients to prescribe and use its products, but it aimed and succeeded in encouraging its targets to take higher doses and use their products for extended periods of time.

Higher doses and long term use raised the bottom line for Purdue, it also raised the risk of addiction and overdose.

However, when patients showed signs of addiction, Purdue urged doctors to respond by increasing the opioid dose, claiming that patients were suffering from "pseudoaddiction" due to underdosing. "By getting patients addicted, Purdue greatly increased patient's risk of harm from many drugs in the opioid class—including heroin [and fentanyl]."[63] Purdue's internal marketing plan focused explicitly on getting patients on higher doses of opioids in order to prolong their use.

According to Massachusetts law, a company's misconduct imposes personal liability on directors and executives given that "(a) they participated in the misconduct; and/or (b) they knew about the misconduct and failed to stop it; and/or (c)

---

62 Ibid.
63 Ibid.

they should have known about the misconduct and they failed to stop it."[64]

In 2007, Purdue Pharma pleaded guilty to a felony crime for misleading doctors and patients about opioids. The company paid $700 million and assured the US government that it would never deceive doctors and patients again.[65]

In 2008, more Americans died from opioid overdoses than ever before.

By 2017, the president of the United States declared the opioid crisis a national public health emergency.

As stated in the lawsuit, "the Defendants' unfair and deceptive conduct continued from this Court's Judgment in May 2007 until 2018."57 Purdue Pharma was able to continue with its misconduct through "in-person sales visits in order to avoid a public paper trail."[66] The "well concealed" strategies Purdue used make it clear that they had no intent on following through with their 2007 promise.[67]

---

64 Ibid.
65 Ibid.
66 Commonwealth of Massachusetts v. Purdue Pharma L.P. (Superior Court Civil Action). Retrieved from https://www.mass.gov/files/documents/2018/06/12/Purdue%20Complaint%20FILED.pdf
67 Ibid.

Purdue Pharma continues to demonstrate that no amount of lives lost is more significant than their profit.

* * *

Lisa Keefe has been a nurse for thirty-three years.

She vividly remembers when opiate medications came on the market.

When it comes to the opioid epidemic, Lisa says, "It is an actual epidemic and no one is immune." These aren't your "quintessential drug dealers, they're your orthopedic surgeons or oral surgeons. They're the ones that are giving you those products. Most people start from the medicine cabinet at home."

* * *

In 2015, Lisa's middle son's best friend died of a heroin overdose. Lisa and a group of other mothers were determined to do something. They started meeting at their local library in Natick, Massachusetts.

Since then, Lisa has attended ten funerals; three of them were that same son's very good friends.

They formed a group. Lisa wasn't sure what it was they were supposed to be doing; her expertise as a nurse was limited. The support group flourished into an advocacy group as the moms got the fire and police departments involved. Natick received a grant to fund a task force specifically for the opioid epidemic.

Natick, Massachusetts, is a wealthy, white town. "We're just regular, normal people," Lisa tells me. "All these kids played sports, came from intact families, their parents were not divorced...it was just shocking."

Lisa attributes her success in Natick to putting the cause out in the open. These women were upstanding mothers of the town, people respected them, so they listened.

Lisa and the other mothers of SOAR (Supporting Outreach and Addiction Recovery) made a significant impact on the community when they brought a survivor of an overdose to the local high school to speak. They offered the students flags to place outside on the lawn, representing a life lost to overdose.

Lisa told me she still gets chills from the student response.

"One thousand seven hundred kids paraded out of the high school, not a word, not a giggle, not a shove, nothing, and planted those flags in the front lawn, and then waited in line again to shake [the speaker›s] hand."

Following the assembly, Lisa was told that roughly a hundred kids came forward saying that they knew someone that struggled with addiction.

* * *

Until further legislative change is enacted, communities such as Lisa's must come together to combat the opioid crisis.

By educating patients on pain management and alternatives to using opioids to treat their pain, communities such as Natick can save lives.

We the people can no longer be taken advantage of by companies seeking to increase their bottom line at the expense of our health and our lives. It ends now.

CHAPTER FOUR

CLOSE TO HOME

I have taken the train on the Chestnut Hill West line down to Suburban Station countless times.

This time, I noticed a few things.

People watching is an extremely interesting activity. I observed the couple in front of me with their matching coffee tumblers, the student with her headphones on and homework in lap, and the woman carrying what seemed to be the entirety of her possessions in three or four bags.

If I look out the window, the stone and brick homes of the suburbs turn to crumbling warehouses, decorated with colorful graffiti and adorned with discarded grocery carts.

As the train approached Suburban Station, the craving for coffee came to me. Stopping in Dunkin› Donuts before heading out onto JFK Boulevard, a woman asked me to buy her a banana. Many men and women have taken refuge in the station in these cold winter months, and a $0.79 banana was the least I could offer this woman.

* * *

As I walk past city hall, dressed for court, nerves set in. I had never been inside the Justice Juanita Kidd Stout Center for Criminal Justice building. Named after Justice Juanita Kidd Stout, who in 1959 became the first African American woman in the state to serve as a judge, the building felt historical as I walked through security and waited for the elevator. I had come to municipal court to sit in on an array of hearings including pretrial bring backs and probation violations.

Arriving in the courtroom on the tenth floor, I was ushered in by an assistant district attorney, seated in the jury box to observe the court's proceedings for the day.

Judge Robert Coleman was already seated at the bench.

Judge Coleman has served the Philadelphia County Court of Common Pleas since 2009. A graduate of Villanova University, his career has been dedicated to serving the public, known for his passion to keep Philadelphians from losing their lives to drug addiction. As I got comfortable in my seat in the jury box, I assessed the room. A full house this Monday morning. I listened intently as a hearing for a violation of probation commenced.

A thirty-two-year-old white man was brought out of custody after spending ninety days in the detention center. He was charged with three counts of theft, one count of burglary, two counts of trespassing, and four counts of receiving stolen property—an accumulation of one felony in the first degree, another in the second degree, and multiple misdemeanors. This individual was addicted to heroin and had committed the preceding crimes to feed his addiction.

Judge Coleman, addressing the defendant, reminded him of his fate: "*You know you're going to die.*"

Holding up a stack of papers, the judge began to read off the names of the men and women whose death certificates had reached his desk in the last few months. As each name was read, the judge threw the certificate behind him, cascading to the floor one by one.

The relatively young man, clearly desperate, sat nervously in his seat. His mother, comforted by a friend, was seated in the courtroom, visibly anxious and crying.

The judge spoke to the defendant, explaining to him that he didn't want to punish him for the disease he was afflicted with.

Judge Coleman is known for his involvement with the County Intermediate Punishment Program, "County IP". Reserved for nonviolent drug offenders, who have committed nonviolent crimes and are dependent upon drugs, the program requires defendants to plead guilty before receiving treatment.

As the defendant was taken back into custody, his mother spoke up, explaining to the Judge that he had committed the theft to be taken back to jail so that he could detox. The man had stolen a bar of soap from a convenience store. The woman, still in tears, thanked the Judge for his extension of the IP program to her son.

* * *

Next, a thirty-year-old white man was brought out after serving time in the Philadelphia Industrial Correctional Center.

In the courtroom for a violation of probation, he had been charged with a felony count of manufacture, delivery or possession with intent to manufacture or deliver, and the possession of a controlled substance.

The defendant had a long history of drug abuse.

The judge reminded the defendant that he was "*just trying to get* [him] *into treatment and keep him alive.*" Judge Coleman is the only judge in the building with an open door policy, meaning that any day of the week, men and women are able to walk into his courtroom if they need more help. The man told the judge he was struggling to obtain his medications for seizures and mental health difficulties. The judge assured him he would be given the proper help to get his medications.

* * *

Next, a thirty-three-year-old black female was pulled from the courtroom crowd. The mother of five, working two jobs, was also appearing for a violation of her probation. Caught on three felony counts of retail theft, a common crime of addicts to feed their addiction, the judge stipulated that if in ninety days the woman was clean, she would not be required to go to treatment, as she had children to take care of at home.

However, the judge reminded the defendant that "in this room, trust is earned, not given." I was amazed by his generosity.

* * *

Next, a twenty-year-old white male was brought out.

The mother of this child was in the courtroom, her hands clasped together as she listened to his sentence.

The defendant appeared due to a violation of his probation. His urine samples had not stayed clean— THC, Benzodiazepines, and Amphetamines were all found. His violation was due to the destruction of his ankle monitor as he was serving time on house arrest.

The defendant explained that he had tripped over a baby gate and accidentally broke the bracelet. He had been in custody for the past month, leaving his child with its mother alone at home.

Judge Coleman was sympathetic, explaining that if the man stayed clean, he would terminate his house arrest. The man was released back to house arrest, the mother of his child looked thrilled.

* * *

The next case was also a violation of probation. A thirty-seven-year-old black male was brought out from custody. Originally arrested for possession and intent to distribute, the man has been sentenced to short term treatment to treat his addiction to heroin and crack cocaine.

The defendant had left treatment, but his parole officer informed the judge that he had returned.

Though the man had been in custody for over a month, Judge Coleman was adamant on keeping him locked up until a bed was ready in treatment to keep him from relapsing.

Judge Coleman vowed, "I will not let you die on my watch. I will not give up on you, don›t give up on me."

* * *

The judge took a break and beckoned to me to join him in the back office. He was warm and friendly, shaking my hand and asking me what I thought of the proceedings.

He shared with me that he was more than willing to work with addicts, even the ones who dealt to support their own addiction. However, he explained, he was not sympathetic to those who smoked pot but dealt heroin.

The judge described those individuals as pure evil, providing the poison that has killed thousands in Philadelphia.

As I inquired about his open door policy, he returned to the bench. The next two appearances were men who had come to the courtroom for that purpose exactly, to ask the judge for help.

* * *

The first was on house arrest. Currently in an intensive outpatient program (IOP) and working, the man was looking to suspend his house arrest so that he could see his father in New Jersey who was sick.

Judge Coleman granted his request.

The next man had completed an inpatient drug treatment program and was also currently in IOP, using methadone as a maintenance drug.

He explained that he had a five-month-old child and was finding it difficult to get a job or go to school as he had a bench warrant on him for not appearing in court previously.

The judge lifted the warrant so that the man could get work and go to school to support his family.

Both of these instances highlighted the Judge's sincere wish to help those who walk into his courtroom. After thanking the judge for allowing me to sit in his courtroom, he invited me back for another set of hearings the coming Thursday.

I came back that Thursday.

* * *

In October, fifty suspects had been arrested in a Kensington drug ring bust.

Among those arrested were individuals accused of controlling the drug enterprise known as the Alameda Drug Trafficking Organization, allegedly selling fentanyl, heroin, cocaine and other drugs that brought in nearly $5 million in annual revenue.

The investigation focused on the intersection of Kip and Cambria Streets, an area known as one of the most dangerous parts of the city.

That day in the courtroom, Judge Coleman was to hear the cases of nineteen of the individuals involved in the bust. The defendants ranged from low-level street dealers to those people who controlled the enterprise. Many of the lower-level dealers were addicts themselves, dealing to support their own addiction.

Judge Coleman explained to me that in his court, "If you're smoking weed, but selling heroin, you're the merchant of death."

* * *

Judge Coleman's time on the bench in Philadelphia has been characterized by his care and concern for the defendants he serves.

After observing his courtroom, I was struck by his candor when speaking with defendants and his passion for my city of Philadelphia.

Throughout each case, Judge Coleman's first priority was doing what was best for the defendant, whether that be treatment, detox, or a spot in his IP program. Before their swearing in, the judge diligently asked each defendant, "How are you doing?" I believe Judge Coleman is a powerful example for the US judicial system. His focus on keeping addicted defendants alive and clean so that they can return to the community and avoid recidivism is essential to changing the way we treat addicts in America. It was an honor to sit in Judge Coleman's courtroom.

* * *

Kensington, Philadelphia, is the largest open-air narcotics market for heroin on the East Coast. Nicknamed the "Walmart of heroin," addicts travel from all over to score in Kensington, and many never leave.[68]

Located off I-95, Kensington Avenue, the neighborhood's main drag, is lined with two-story row houses, pawn shops, and Irish pubs.

Kensington is known for having both the cheapest and purest heroin in the region.

The heroin in Kensington used to be pure enough to snort, but has recently been mixed with fentanyl.

Fentanyl is a synthetic opioid used to treat severe pain. It is fifty to one hundred times more potent than morphine, according to the CDC. The fentanyl found in heroin is likely illegally made, non pharmaceutical, and not prescribed. In Philadelphia, deaths related to fentanyl have increased by 95 percent in the past year. The city's Department of Health estimates that seventy-five thousand residents are addicted to heroin and other opioids. According to *The New York Times*,

---

68 Percy, J. (2018, October 10). Trapped by the 'Walmart of Heroin'. *The New York Times*. Retrieved from https://www.nytimes.com/2018/10/10/magazine/kensington-heroin-opioid-philadelphia.html

Philadelphia County has the highest overdose rate of any of the ten most populous counties in America.[69]

* * *

Heroin has built an entire tent city under Philadelphia's elevated train tracks, known as the El.

With nowhere else to go, addicts began setting up camp.

Entire communities filled a full city block with homeless addicts. Drug overdoses have become the third leading cause of death in Philadelphia, behind heart disease and cancer.

In the fall of 2018, Philadelphia Mayor Jim Kenney signed an executive order declaring an opioid disaster in Kensington. "The crisis has created unacceptable conditions for Kensington and the surrounding neighborhood," the executive order reads. "Nearly 150 people are camped on Frankford Avenue and Emerald Street, alone, with smaller encampments spread throughout the community. Drugs are bought, sold, and injected openly. Addiction has increased the number of individuals participating in the sex trade. Streets, school yards and public parks are littered with trash, human waste

---

69   Ibid.

and used syringes. Children and commuters dodge illegal activity on their way to school and work."[70]

The city has tried expanding outreach and education efforts in Kensington, including by creating homeless outreach teams, distributing Naloxone (Narcan) to community groups, and cleaning illegal dumping sites, but it's just not enough. In fact, the city's motives are questionable. As property values in Kensington have begun to rise, city resources have increased. The city essentially ignored Kensington for as long as possible, now, trying to use temporary fixes to solve a potentially unsolvable problem.

The narrative of the opioid crisis is focused on Big Pharma greed, but in Kensington, the reality is far more complicated. Many people first came to Kensington because a car accident or surgery had left them addicted to painkillers. Later, when they could no longer afford them, they graduated to heroin.

Getting those in Kensington into treatment is close to impossible.

When the city evacuated the tent cities under the El, they offered treatment, but most of the addicts didn't accept

---

70 Philadelphia, Executive Office of the Mayor [James Kenney]. Executive Order No. 3-18: Opioid Emergency Response Executive Order. https://www.phila.gov/ExecutiveOrders/Executive%20Orders/eo099318.pdf

it. Instead, they moved into abandoned buildings and crumbling churches. In a *New York Times* article, one addict said "people think we are having fun down here. Are you insane? I live under a bridge."[71]

Then why aren't addicts taking the treatment that is being offered by the city?

Opioid withdrawal is worse than the possibility of arrest, overdose, or death.

Addicts use to avoid "getting sick," or withdrawing. This leads to an increase in crime rates in places like Kensington, according to Ben Naish, commanding officer of the Northeast Division for the Philadelphia Police.

Officer Naish joined the Philadelphia Police Department in the early '90s following the crack cocaine epidemic in America, affecting predominantly black, impoverished communities. He has witnessed this "dangerous, devastating cycle" for many years on the force, and commiserates with me about the number of lives and families ruined as well as the rate at which Americans are dying to the disease of addiction.

---

71 Percy, J. (2018, October 10). Trapped by the 'Walmart of Heroin'. *The New York Times*. Retrieved from https://www.nytimes.com/2018/10/10/magazine/kensington-heroin-opioid-philadelphia.html

Officer Naish told me that property crime is the main problem the police are facing in Kensington. Addicts will break into cars or steal computers to sell items and continue to feed their addiction. Auto theft, retail theft, and prostitution are all drug fueled crimes in the city of Philadelphia.

From a professional standpoint, Officer Naish says it is frustrating to see the impact addiction has on the community he serves. However, he adds, that every American knows someone affected by addiction, which makes the issue personal for him.

In Philadelphia, it is not uncommon for members of the Philly PD to be directly affected by the disease of addiction. Officer Valerie Felici has been a police officer for seventeen years in Philadelphia. Her husband is also an officer on the force. Her twenty-five-year-old son has been battling a heroin addiction for seven years.

Valerie experiences addiction both as a police officer and as a mother. She has started an outreach group in the Philadelphia counties to connect with people on the streets who are addicted and hopefully get them into treatment. Philadelphia is greatly impacted by heroin, and just recently fentanyl has been introduced into the city.

Fentanyl use in Philadelphia has grown due to its distribution among drug dealers. Many users were unaware that there was fentanyl in their heroin. Therefore, when users would use pure heroin, not laced with fentanyl, they would still feel sick, it would not cure the craving and withdrawal symptoms.

Val tells me there's only a few corners left in the East Division selling actual heroin.

This discovery is dangerous, and personal for Val. Her son has been in treatment over forty times, and has spent the last few months living on the streets. "He was in rehab," Val told me. "He left, he called me and said, 'I'm sorry I left, please come help me.' So I went and got him and sent him somewhere else." However, Val's son left again, and she couldn't locate him until a few girls from her outreach group went looking for him. When they found him, he was unwilling to come with them. However, the girls insisted he take Narcan, a nasal spray that reverses an opioid overdose.

Thank God he did. He had been on the street for three days when he heard someone scream "Who has Narcan!?" There was a girl overdosing and he was able to save her. It is quite common now for other addicts to carry the miracle drug for this purpose exactly.

* * *

Val remembers when her son would come home from keg parties, where he was doing "normal teenage stuff." However, she shared, "By the time I realized that it was more than just the alcohol, you know, we were already into the heroin. It was absolutely devastating because in my mind, I'm looking at it two ways: my child is an addict. Oh my God, what the hell do I do? And then I›m looking at it as a police officer, and I'm like, oh my God, my child›s an addict. You know. It's a whole different world because we see the bad parts of addiction. We see that on a routine basis. The quality of life, crimes that come with it, living on the streets. It's the stigma, the stigma of, oh my God, he's going to be homeless....he's gonna lose his teeth. He's going to be dirty...because that's the stigma of addiction."

Val admits that she didn't understand addiction yet. She felt she wasn't getting what she needed to be able to help her son get what he needed. So she started reading and educating herself.

"When it came to addiction, I was reading all day long, just every chance I could get, finding new articles, anybody that I could speak to that had any kind of knowledge on addiction. I'm still doing that to this day, you know, every day I'm online looking for new information that's out there and ways that I can help."

Valeri›s persistence to save her son has benefitted many other Philadelphians in the process.

However, Val says it was hard to ask for help with her son as a police officer. "We're not supposed to be the ones asking for help, we›re supposed to be the ones helping people."

As a mother, her son's addiction affected her in its own way. Val says the loved ones of an addict must recover too. She tells me, "We have our own recovery process because we have gone through this emotional roller coaster." For Valerie, being a police officer is an emotional, rational thing. Valerie's profession made her realize that her "action [could] make a huge impact on whether [a] person›s gonna live or die." "So you really have to act as fast as possible," Val told me, "it's very emotional."

Val promised me that there were many people like her out in the world fighting for change. "One of my favorite things to do is when we go to the recovery houses, cheer on the people that are actually in recovery because I feel like sometimes they get forgotten...but they still need support." Valerie along with other mothers go and cook for a few recovery houses. "We go in there and we cook food and we give them makeup bags. It just kind of helps them feel a little bit more confident about themselves...such a difference. A hug can make such a difference," Val says.

* * *

To further understand the efforts being made to combat the crisis in Philadelphia, I reached out to Brian Abernathy, the managing director of the city of Philadelphia. Appointed by Mayor Kenney in January 2019, Director Abernathy is the brain behind the Philadelphia Resilience Project.

As the city continued to exhaust its emergency resources, Brian told me his staff was "overwhelmed," which led to a realization. "We needed to think and work differently." To Brian, that meant the partnership of thirty-five city departments to combat the opioid epidemic, creating the Resilience Project. The project identified seven key mission areas:

- clearing major encampments

- reducing criminal activity

- reducing homeless population

- reducing trash and litter

- reducing overdoses and spread of infectious disease

- increasing treatment options

- mobilizing community resources

Director Abernathy and the Resilience Project face a unique issue in Kensington: both the addicts' and the residents' needs must be met. Brian explained that the first three months of the project focused on stabilizing the community; the next stage was to create and analyze better data so that progress could be charted.

It was important that Brian and his team's success didn't depend solely on the decrease of deaths in Kensington. However, it is difficult to get active addicts into treatment. They may not have a form of ID, may not be ready emotionally, and may not want to go through withdrawal.

Staff engagement with addicts in the area is crucial. Brian described to me a recent encounter where staff approached five people on the street; two accepted literature, one walked away, and two accepted treatment. This outreach is progress. It's hard work.

Brian says every time he walks through Kensington he can see the "devastation of the disease." Over the past few months, debate has begun in regard to opening a safe injection site in Kensington. Safe injection sites are medically supervised facilities designed to provide a hygienic and stress-free environment in which individuals are able to consume illicit recreational drugs intravenously and reduce nuisance from public drug use.

The United States Department of Justice has filed a civil lawsuit against the nonprofit organization Safehouse in Philadelphia in February 2019 to prevent its opening. The nonprofit Safehouse filed a countersuit against the US government arguing its proposed operation is a "legitimate medical intervention, not illicit drug dens."

Director Abernathy says safe injections sites "go against everything he was raised to believe in." Though he doesn't like the idea, he says "it's the only way I can keep people alive." He says the mayor is supportive of the site as well.

Brian told me that his office traveled to Vancouver, Canada, to see how they instituted safe injection sites into their communities. He found that advocacy was key, Kensington would need both addicts and residents to champion the site, but that would require education, a comprehensive safety protocol, the support of the police commissioner and the district attorney.

Director Abernathy is "confident that [Philadelphia] has some of the best programs in the country, but they are still not good enough." Treatment needs to be longer, more attractive, and more successful.

When I asked what's next for Philadelphia, Brain told me the mayor's emergency declaration, which was set to expire June

2019, will likely be extended. Great work has been done, but there is still work to do.

The city of Philadelphia needs long-term sustainability. Without a unified force in the city government, the crisis will continue.

CHAPTER FIVE

THE LAW FAILS US

———

Misti started taking Oxycontin to help with the pain of her scoliosis when she was a teenager.

After becoming addicted, she traveled to Seattle to find large quantities of the drug and found heroin instead.

For the next seven years, she struggled with addiction, living between a tent and a jail cell, racking up charges for possession and prostitution.

According to the American Civil Liberties Union (ACLU), almost thirty thousand people were arrested for drugs in

New York in 2012. Over 117,000 people were arrested in California the same year.[72]

Many of these offenders, like Misti, have been arrested multiple times—their addictions untreated while behind bars.

This cycle continues to repeat itself.

* * *

In the United States, jails and prisons are full.

Though the United States accounts for 5 percent of the world's population, it houses 25 percent of the world's prison population. The United States is incarcerating its citizens at a disproportionate rate. The swell in the US prison population is a relatively new phenomenon. Between the years 1920 and 1970, 110 out of one hundred thousand people in the United States were imprisoned. However, that number skyrocketed in 1970 to roughly 714 out of one hundred thousand.[73]

---

72 Dansky, K., Senior Counsel. (2014, October 17). Jail Doesn't Help Addicts. Let's Stop Sending Them There. Retrieved from American Civil Liberties Union website: https://www.aclu.org/blog/smart-justice/mass-incarceration/jail-doesnt-help-addicts-lets-stop-sending-them-there

73 Hines, Regan, dir. *Incarcerating Us.* 2016.

The election of Richard Nixon in 1969 drastically changed the goal of the US prison system from rehabilitation to punishment. Nixon's declaration of a war on drugs prompted influential legislation that ultimately led to the increase in the United States' prison population. This "war" included an increase in federal spending, new congressional laws, and the creation of the Drug Enforcement Administration (DEA).[74]

Time, effort, money, and plenty of politics contributed to the problems the prison system is facing today. Prisons are no longer the penitentiaries originally designed for criminals to seek "penance" or atonement, but a means by which the government can remove those they deem unfavorable to society.

Prisons now serve as mental health facilities, hospitals, and schools, services the Department of Justice is not equipped to administer. According to Criminal Justice Policy Foundation founder, Robert Linnell, "The war on drugs was a mistake and counterproductive."[75]

The Department of Justice should be focused on violent and dangerous crimes. Nonviolent drug crime offenders, highly targeted since the election of Nixon, take resources and focus away from murders, rapes, and robberies. The effects of the war on

---

74 Ibid.
75 Ibid.

drugs have upended the country for roughly forty years and the laws we have set into place have failed us. Mandatory minimum sentencing laws were and still are a tactic that the government has used to further the original goal of the war on drugs: to live in a drug free society. However, in 2018, drug overdoses are the leading cause of death for Americans under the age of fifty.

The war on drugs has failed and Americans are dying and being locked up because of it.

* * *

The city of Seattle is trying something different.

Since 2012, the city's Law Enforcement Assisted Diversion program (LEAD) has worked to put more addicts in treatment than jail. Instead of locking people struggling with addiction up, officers connect addicts directly with the treatment and services they need to help get them sober.[76]

Instead of wasting time and money with a court hearing and saddling people with a criminal record, LEAD doesn't waste time. In addition, unlike drug courts, LEAD participants who relapse are not threatened with jail time and expulsion from the program.

76 LEAD Law Enforcement Assisted Diversion. (n.d.). Retrieved from http://leadkingcounty.org

The United States has been waging a failed war on drugs, drug use hasn›t gone down. Instead of finding solutions to addiction in the United States, we've created a society that seemingly disregards millions of lives—particularly the lives of black and brown Americans.

Locking addicts up—especially for egregious periods of time—does not help them. It's time the United States buys into a system of treatment, rather than punishment.

* * *

In 2001, the ACLU published a paper titled "Prison Overpopulation & Harsh Sentencing," stating that "restrictive sentencing guidelines and statutory mandatory minimum sentences have taken away the discretion of judges to tailor sentences to fit the individual circumstances of particular crimes and offenders. Thus the traditional requirement mandated by the Eighth Amendment that punishment maintain some proportion to the crime committed has been abandoned in the name of the ‹war on drugs.'"[77]

---

77 American Civil Liberties Union (ACLU). "Have Mandatory Minimum Jail Sentences Been an Effective Tool in the War on Drugs?" ACLU Pros & Cons. Last modified November 11, 2009. https://aclu. procon.org/view.answers.php?questionID=000727.

The ACLU has been a consistent liberal and powerful voice in this debate and brings an important perspective to the conversation: that of judges. Since Congress expanded the use of mandatory minimum sentencing statutes in the 1980s, federal judges have protested them as an "unwarranted intrusion"[78] upon their authority. For example, the Judicial Conference has continuously registered its opposition in its reports to Congress.

In a 2011 opinion, Senior Judge Jack Weinstein in the Eastern District of New York warned that mandatory minimum sentences "impose grave costs not only on the punished but on the moral credibility upon which our system of criminal justice depends."[79]

Judge Weinstein is not alone in his dissent for mandatory minimums.

"In most of the over 1,000 congressionally-mandated mandatory minimum sentences that I have imposed over the past twenty-two years," wrote Iowa Judge Mark Bennett in a 2015 opinion, "I have stated on the record that they were unjust and too harsh."[80]

---

78 Roth, Jessica A. "The 'New' District Court Activism in Criminal Justice Reform." *New York University Annual Survey of American Law*, 2018.
79 Ibid.
80 Ibid.

Judge Bennett has written extensively about the need for reform, which is uncommon for a federal judge to do.

"Federal judges have a longstanding culture of not speaking out on issues of public concern," Bennett explains.[81]

Judge Bennett attributes his outspokenness on the issue to the "daily grist"[82] of unjust mandatory minimum sentencing for nonviolent drug offenders.

In contrast to many federal judges, proponents of mandatory minimum sentences continue to defend the statute. In 2007, Richard Roper III, former US attorney for the Northern District of Texas, testified before the US House Subcommittee on Crime, Terrorism, and Homeland Security of the Judiciary Committee stating that "mandatory sentencing systems work" and that "the Department [would remain] committed to the principles that gave rise to mandatory sentencing in the first place—consistency, fairness, certainty, truth, and greater justice in sentencing."[83]

---

81 Ibid.
82 Ibid.
83 American Civil Liberties Union (ACLU). "Have Mandatory Minimum Jail Sentences Been an Effective Tool in the War on Drugs?" ACLU Pros & Cons. Last modified November 11, 2009.https://aclu. procon.org/view.answers.php?questionID=000727.

Politics seems to play a significant factor in the defense of mandatory minimums, as politicians feel they need to appeal to voters, despite widespread support for repeal from distinguished individuals and groups.

For example, the American Bar Association (ABA) stated in 2009 that "[The ABA] supports the repeal of all mandatory minimum statutes and the expanded use of alternatives to incarceration for nonviolent offenders."[84] This statement comes years after US Supreme Court Justice Anthony Kennedy urged the association to speak out against mandatory minimums in a speech at the ABA annual meeting in August of 2003.[85] Agencies such as the DEA also have weighed in on the issue, arguing that "mandatory minimum sentences can...incapacitate dangerous offenders for long periods of time, thereby increasing public safety."[86]

While the conversation has grown, hope for reform seems to be within reach thanks to the efforts of former President

---

84 American Civil Liberties Union (ACLU). "Have Mandatory Minimum Jail Sentences Been an Effective Tool in the War on Drugs?" ACLU Pros & Cons. Last modified November 11, 2009. https://aclu.procon.org/view.answers.php?questionID=000727.

85 American Bar Association. "Mandatory Minimums in the Federal System." *Human Rights Magazine*, October 3, 2012.

86 American Civil Liberties Union (ACLU). "Have Mandatory Minimum Jail Sentences Been an Effective Tool in the War on Drugs?" ACLU Pros & Cons. Last modified November 11, 2009. https://aclu.procon.org/view.answers.php?questionID=000727.

Obama and the growing public awareness of mass incarceration and mandatory minimums.

* * *

In 1994, twenty-four-year-old Kemba Smith was sentenced to 24.5 years in prison for her participation in her boyfriend's illegal drug activities. She had no criminal record, and she was seven months pregnant.

According to the Sentencing Project, Kemba Smith was raised in a protective, middle-class community near Richmond, Virginia. In 1989, Smith, a nineteen-year-old sophomore at Hampton University, met Peter Hall. She spent four years in an abusive relationship with Hall, who was eight years older and, unbeknownst to Smith, the leader of a $4 million crack cocaine ring and one of the FBI's 15 Most Wanted.

Smith attempted to leave Hall multiple times, who abused her physically and emotionally. Their relationship was a tumultuous one, and when Hall was discovered murdered, the government held Smith accountable for the total amount of the drugs in his conspiracy charge.

"I did not traffic drugs, but I knew my boyfriend did. I knew while living with him that he did not have a job and we were living off of the proceeds of his drug crimes. I never claimed total innocence and this is the reason why I pled guilty," Smith testified before the Inter-American Commission on Human Rights in 2006.[87]

Due to mandatory minimum sentencing guidelines, the court was unable to take into consideration the fact that Smith had participated in Hall's illegal activities, such as delivering money to his associates, out of fear for her life. Despite being a first-time, nonviolent offender, Smith was sentenced to twenty-four years in prison.

* * *

Mandatory minimum sentencing laws have been misused by the Department of Justice for many years. They are frequently directed against low-level offenders, contrary to the original intent of Congress. In partnership with sentencing guidelines, most sentences in the past thirty years have been "unjustly long for the conduct and culpability of the defendant."[88]

Mandatory minimum laws have essentially removed the authority from federal judges and relied on the quantity and type of drug involved in the case. "The elimination of judicial

87 Kemba Smith. (n.d.). Retrieved from The Sentencing Project website: https://www.sentencingproject.org/stories/kemba-smith/

88 "Mandatory Minimums and Sentencing Reform." Criminal Justice Policy Foundation. https://www.cjpf.org/mandatory-minimums/#.

discretion in sentencing has allowed prosecutors to acquire excessive power to impose sentences."[89] As explained by the Criminal Justice Policy Foundation, "defendants who plan to assert a legal defense (guaranteed by the U.S. Constitution) are threatened by prosecutors that they will inform the court that the defendants are failing to 'take responsibility.' A finding of failing to take responsibility results in longer sentences."[90] For this reason, mandatory minimums have swelled the federal prison population and in turn led to egregious racial disparities.

Extreme politics have also contributed to the institution of mandatory minimums. The Anti-Drug Abuse Act of 1986 was the legislation that changed the US prison system from a rehabilitative system to a punitive system. After Len Bias, a University of Maryland basketball star, died of a cocaine overdose, Congress became emotionally motivated to mobilize. In July of 1986, four months before the midterm election, Representative Thomas O'Neill Jr., speaker of the house, began asking committees, even those not related to drugs, to contribute to the passage of legislation to be brought to the floor after labor day. The mandatory minimum laws included in the bill were designed to deter would-be criminals

---

89 Ibid.
90 Ibid.

and incapacitate violators. They were also enacted to promote uniform punishment.

Mandatory minimums are not a new concept to the US government. There were uniform punishments since 1776, for crimes including piracy, bank robberies, and skyjacking. However, the mandatory minimum laws for drug crimes were prompted solely by the headlines reporting on the crack cocaine epidemic in the 1980s.

Mandatory minimums were never supposed to encourage and exacerbate America's drug problem but, unfortunately, they did. Federal drug laws, substantially revised by the Anti-Drug Abuse Act of 1986, carry very long maximum sentences—up to forty years for some quantities, and up to life imprisonment for somewhat larger quantities.

"The Anti-Drug Abuse Act of 1986 also required a minimum sentence of 5 years for drug offenses that involved 5 grams of crack, 500 grams of cocaine, 1 kilogram of heroin, 40 grams of a substances with a detectable amount of fentanyl, 5 grams of methamphetamine, 100 kilograms or 100 plants of marijuana, and other drugs. That law also required a minimum sentence of 10 years for drug offenses that involved 50 grams of crack, 5 kilograms of cocaine, 10 kilograms of heroin, 400 grams of a substance with a detectable amount of fentanyl, 50 grams of methamphetamine, 1000 kilograms or 1000 plants of marijuana, and other drugs."[91]

Essentially, Congress abandoned the idea that federal judges could appropriately identify and punish the most serious drug offenders.

The transfer of sentencing power from judges to prosecutors has significantly contributed to the growth of the US federal prison system. Prosecutors frequently threaten defendants into plea bargains through the prospect of longer sentences. "As a result, every year at least 95 percent of federal drug defendants plead guilty."[92] These "behind-closed-doors"[93] deals leave room for prosecutorial misconduct and incentivize both prosecutors and police officers to arrest and convict to further their own careers. Similarly to what was done in the era of alcohol prohibition, the United States government has simply decided that millions of Americans are criminals.

Conspiracy laws have also deeply impacted the way the federal prison system punishes defendants. In a drug-related crime, "mandatory minimum punishments are based on

91   "Mandatory Minimums and Sentencing Reform." Criminal Justice Policy Foundation. https://www.cjpf.org/mandatory-minimums/#.
92   Ibid.
93   Hines, Regan, dir. *Incarcerating Us*. 2016.

the total weight of drugs of all transactions all the persons who are part of the conspiracy are alleged to have carried out, and not on the individual defendant's actual level of involvement. Thus, a single-trip drug courier faces the same penalty as the ringleader who arranged all the shipments of the organization."[94] These laws result in disparities between low-level and truly high-level offenders.

According to the Criminal Justice Policy Foundation, methamphetamine offenders "face a minimum five-year sentence for distribution of five grams, the weight of five Sweet-n-Low(R) packets, when a heavy user might go through a gram in a day. A genuine high-level trafficker arranges multiple shipments of hundreds of kilograms. In addition, all the non-drug ingredients of a drug shipment are counted in the weight. 500 grams of 50% pure cocaine is counted as 500 grams of cocaine, not 250 grams."[95] These firm sentencing guidelines affixed to mandatory minimums are counterproductive to Congress's goal of punishing high-level offenders and instead punish the average user who might require treatment.

---

94 "Mandatory Minimums and Sentencing Reform." Criminal Justice Policy Foundation. https://www.cjpf.org/mandatory-minimums/#.

95 "Mandatory Minimums and Sentencing Reform." Criminal Justice Policy Foundation. https://www.cjpf.org/mandatory-minimums/#.

In 2011, the US Sentencing Commission reported that "high-level" suppliers or importers made up only 10.9 percent of federal defendants. Wholesalers of any amount made up 21.2 percent, street level dealers 17.2 percent, and couriers -23 percent of people sentenced for drug offenses. Only 2.2 percent were managers or supervisors. The rest of federal drug defendants were other low-level offenders, even marginally involved friends and family of the accused.[96]

The effect of mandatory minimum sentencing laws has reached every corner of the United States, socially, economically, and politically. Excessive and disproportionate sentences are not only unjust but extremely expensive and wasteful. In fiscal year 2015, the average cost of incarceration of a federal prisoner was just under $32,000. The federal prison budget has risen from less than $3.7 billion in 2000 to $7 billion in 2017.[97] These laws also greatly affect US society. "They harm 5 million children who have or have had a parent in prison—including one in nine black children."[98] They waste human potential and economic prosperity. The formerly incarcerated population not only has trouble being

96 Judicial Branch United States Sentencing Committee. *Mandatory Minimum Penalties for Drug Offenses in the Federal System.* N.p., 2017.
97 "Mandatory Minimums and Sentencing Reform." Criminal Justice Policy Foundation. https://www.cjpf.org/mandatory-minimums/#.
98 Gertner, Nancy, and Chiraag Bains. "Mandatory Minimum Sentences Are Cruel and Ineffective. Sessions Wants Them Back." *The Washington Post*, May 15, 2017.

hired, but also with being paid as much as employees with no criminal record. It contributes to a cyclical pattern of children of those imprisoned also committing and being convicted of a crime.

* * *

Kemba Smith's egregious sentence in 1994 kept her from raising her son. "My burden," Smith says, "is that I represent the thousands of others still currently incarcerated; some are my friends who I left behind that deserve an opportunity to raise their children."[99]

More than 60 percent of women in state prisons have a child under the age of eighteen.[100]

The number of women with excessive prison sentences, including Kemba Smith, as a result of their affiliations with male counterparts has rapidly increasing. Many women refuse to testify against their spouses and partners. In addition, more than half of the women in state prisons have suffered physical or sexual abuse.

99 Kemba Smith. (n.d.). Retrieved from The Sentencing Project website: https://www.sentencingproject.org/stories/kemba-smith/
100 Kemba Smith. (n.d.). Retrieved from The Sentencing Project website: https://www.sentencingproject.org/stories/kemba-smith/

Smith's story gained nationwide attention and was featured in campaigns to expose the inadequacy of US drug policy. Smith's parents, who were raising her son while she was incarcerated, were tireless in seeking clemency for their daughter.

After spending six and a half years in prison, Smith was granted clemency in December 2000 by President Clinton.

* * *

In 2017, the US Sentencing Commission reported on the use and impact of mandatory minimum penalties, finding that mandatory minimum sentences continue to result in longer sentences, continue to grow the federal prison population, and have been used more broadly than Congress may have originally anticipated.

* * *

In 2007, Brian Gall, a college student at the University of Iowa, was involved in a drug ring distributing ecstasy.

He later left the drug conspiracy and moved to Arizona, where he started his own business and led a crime-free life.

When federal agents found him, he turned himself in and pleaded guilty to conspiracy to distribute a controlled substance. The state argued for a sentence of thirty months in prison, which was the minimum sentence recommended for the offense by the federal sentencing guidelines. In considering all the mitigating circumstances in Gall's case, the judge instead decided to abandon the guidelines and impose a sentence of thirty-six months of probation.

The US Court of Appeals for the Eighth Circuit rejected the below-guidelines sentence as unreasonable, holding that "while the guidelines are not mandatory, sentences that fall outside of the recommended sentencing range must overcome a presumption of unreasonableness."[101] The Eighth Circuit ruled that the district court had made a mistake in using Gall's youth as a mitigating factor, overestimating his rehabilitation and understating the seriousness of his crime. Since the "extraordinary variance" was not justified by a finding of extraordinary circumstances, the Eighth Circuit ordered a new sentence.

The US Supreme Court heard Brian Gall's case and ruled 7-2 in favor, reversing the appellate court. The majority opinion, delivered by Justice Kennedy, held, under *U.S. v. Booker,* that federal courts have the authority to set reasonable sentences

---

101 Brian Michael Gall v. United States, No. 128 S.Ct. 586 (Dec. 10, 2007).

so long as they provide an explanation. The Court clarified that *Booker* removed the guidelines from their earlier status as the primary determinant of a defendant's punishment and instead granted them advisory status. *Gall v. U.S.* is an excellent example of the constrictions placed upon the US court system, which in turn affects the prison system and the nation as a whole.

The district court judge's decision to grant a lower sentence of thirty-six months of probation was subjectively fair and reasonable, considering the mitigating factors of the case. However, due to mandatory minimum sentencing laws, Brian Gall did not receive a fair sentence.

Mandatory minimums not only remove the authority of a judge and rely on fixed sentences, but remove the human aspect of sentencing. Uniform sentencing, especially in drug crimes, eliminates the consideration of the defendant as a human being, a citizen, a father, mother or child. In repealing mandatory minimums, the government would grant federal judges the ability to sentence defendants as they see appropriate and proportionate, creating a fair and just judicial system for all Americans.

* * *

As the United States aches from the damages they have suffered due to the war on drugs and legislation such as mandatory minimums, activists are fighting for reform in our criminal justice system. "'New' activist district court judges have pushed the limits of their supervisory and persuasive authority to create local diversionary programs and alternatives to incarceration,"[102] reports the American Bar Association. Alternatives that seek to divert offenders from incarceration and direct them to "drug treatment or other services and counseling...successful completion of these programs usually will result in the individual facing no prison time, and often emerging with no criminal record."

Since 1989, many state courts have instituted such alternative programs, and the number has continued to grow. In 2013, there were seven such programs among the ninety-four federal districts; as of 2016, that number had more than tripled to twenty-two.[103] In many districts, trial judges have been leading the fight for these programs.

As Judge Stefan Underhill of Connecticut, who championed the effort in Connecticut, explained, "I had been a judge long enough that I had become frustrated with the revolving

---

102 American Bar Association. "Mandatory Minimums in the Federal System." *Human Rights Magazine*, October 3, 2012.

103 American Bar Association. "Mandatory Minimums in the Federal System." *Human Rights Magazine*, October 3, 2012.

door," i.e., sentencing those with drug addiction to prison, only to see them later reoffend because they did not receive treatment."[104] Lower court judges have also brought attention to the consequences of criminal convictions and the inaccessibility to obtain employment, housing, and education. Convicted felons are also precluded from voting or protecting noncitizens from deportation.

Mass incarceration, partnered with such laws pertaining to former convicts, has greatly affected people of color in the United States. These "collateral consequences"[105] have recently gained public attention through popular books such as Michelle Alexander's *The New Jim Crow: Mass Incarceration in the Age of Colorblindness.*

* * *

Great strides have been made toward the repeal of mandatory minimums and the long-awaited reform of the US criminal justice system. In 2017, when President Donald Trump was elected, it was unclear whether legislation for criminal justice reform would prevail in Congress. Proponent of mandatory minimum sentencing laws, Attorney General Jeff Sessions had brought those who shared his view into senior leadership

---

104 Ibid.
105 Ibid.

at the Department of Justice, including Jared Kushner, son-in-law of President Trump, who had been meeting with senators about sentencing reform.

By the end of 2017, there was no legislative progress. In November 2018, President Trump announced his support behind a substantial revision of the nation's prison and sentencing laws, developed by a bipartisan group of senators called the First Step Act. The First Step Act was "overwhelmingly"[106] passed in the Senate on December 18, 2018.

The FSA "would expand job training and other programming aimed at reducing recidivism rates among federal prisoners. It also expands early-release programs and modifies sentencing laws, including mandatory minimum sentences for non-violent drug offenders, to more equitably punish drug offenders."[107] The bill is set to pass in the House as well, and President Trump has said he would sign the bill.

Though not the expansive overhaul proposed originally by the Obama administration, the First Step Act is an important "first step" for the unlikely coalition of liberals and conservatives the US government needs to reform its broken criminal justice system.

---

106 Fandos, Nicholas. "Senate Passes Bipartisan Criminal Justice Bill." *The New York Times*, December 18, 2018.
107 Ibid.

However, we can do more.

According to the US Federal Bureau of Prisons, 46.0 percent of inmates are incarcerated for drug offenses. The United States, suffering from mass incarceration and increasing overdose deaths, is in need of a solution.

A conversation about whether the answer is the legalization or decriminalization of all drugs has become prominent throughout the government, advocacy groups, and citizens across the nation. However, this issue prevailed for years prior. Reformers have been calling for an end to the aggressive use of the criminal justice system to control drug use for many years, pointing to issues of racial inequality, startling costs and ineffectiveness.

In 1966, California became the first state to allow doctors to recommend medical marijuana for qualifying patients, most notably those diagnosed with cancer. Since then, twenty states and Washington, D.C., have enacted similar statutes. In 2012, Colorado and Washington voters passed ballot initiatives legalizing marijuana use for the general adult population, provided that the state would regulate, tax, and control its sale as it does with alcohol and cigarettes.

The relaxation upon marijuana in the United States has prompted conversation about other illegal drugs. The legalization of marijuana at the state level could encourage Americans to push to legalize all drugs in an effort to assist addicts and curb mass incarceration.

However, decriminalization might be the answer Americans are looking for, as it has been adopted worldwide.

* * *

In 2001, Portugal decriminalized the "acquisition, possession, and use of small quantities of all psychoactive drugs... including heroin and cocaine."[108]

Though Portugal admits many shortcomings of this legislation, its effect upon the Portuguese population was significant.

Hannah Laqueur states in her 2015 article "Uses and Abuses of Drug Decriminalization in Portugal" that the law did not legalize drugs or alter the "criminal penalty prohibiting the production, distribution, and sale of drugs." Rather, the law

---

108 Hannah Laqueur, "ARTICLE: Uses and Abuses of Drug Decriminalization in Portugal," *Law & Social Inquiry,* 40, 746 (Summer, 2015). https://advance.lexis.com/api/document?collection=analytical-materials&id=urn:contentItem:5GWF-G0S0-00CV-S1GD-00 000-00&context=1516831.

decriminalized drug use: "acts of acquisition, possession, and consumption."[109]

Portugal's reforms were not the only movement on this issue. Both Spain and Italy "ceased imposing criminal sanctions for possession of small quantities of any psychoactive substances decades ago." In addition, Mexico "enacted legislation in 2009 that removed the criminal penalties for anyone possessing small amounts of marijuana, cocaine, heroin, and methamphetamine."[110]

Previously to Portugal's 2001 legislation, fines served as the primary penalty for individuals arrested and convicted of drug use. Less than one percent of those incarcerated for a drug offense were imprisoned. The most notable change in Portugal following 2001 was in the court system in regard to its practices regarding a shift from a "penal to therapeutic approach to drug abuse."[111]

* * *

---

109 Hannah Laqueur, "ARTICLE: Uses and Abuses of Drug Decriminalization in Portugal," *Law & Social Inquiry,* 40, 746 (Summer, 2015). https://advance.lexis.com/api/document?collection=analytical-materials&id=urn:contentItem:5GWF-G0S0-00CV-S1GD-00 000-00&context=1516831.

110 Ibid.

111 Ibid.

In the United States, most organizations that support the legalization of marijuana also advocate for broader drug law repeals. Beginning in the 1990s, drug courts were established to divert users from the criminal justice system into treatment. "These diversion programs, unlike the system developed in Portugal, remain part of the criminal justice system." Including such programs in the criminal justice system continues to perpetuate imprisonment, as a user's failure to comply can result in their conviction.

The question Laqueur poses is if the aim of decriminalization to treat rather than punish drug use.

While decriminalization addresses the United States's addiction and overdose death crisis, it ignores the occasional user who does not require treatment. Legalization solves this tension, according to Laqueur. "If the United States were to adopt a decriminalization statute like Portugal's, the impact might be considerable," claims Laqueur. "Roughly 80 percent of drug arrests in the United States are for possession...5 to 15 percent of those in prison for a drug offense are there for possession rather than distribution-related charges." A US decriminalization statute could have the power to decrease substance abuse and addiction rates, as Portugal experienced. Individuals with a substance abuse disorder are more likely to find recovery in rehab than in jail. In addition, addiction treatment is less expensive than incarceration. To enact such a statute, the United

States would be required to invest in treatment and rehabilitation, moving away from its "tough on crime" precedents.

* * *

Despite the fairly new understanding of addiction as a public health crisis, the United States continues to lock up Americans for drug related crimes. The US prison system is a profitable market; therefore, more prisoners contribute to a bigger bottom line.

A trend the ACLU and other advocacy organizations have taken on is the school-to-prison pipeline. The ACLU describes the school-to-prison pipeline as "a disturbing national trend wherein children are funneled out of public schools and into the juvenile and criminal justice systems."[112]

"Zero-tolerance" policies criminalize minor infractions of school rules, resulting in detention, suspension, or expulsion. These policies have resulted in disproportionate punishment for black students.

According to the ACLU, "while black students only make up 16% of public school enrollment, they account for 42% of all

112 School-To-Prison Pipeline. (n.d.). Retrieved from American Civil Liberties Union website: https://www.aclu.org/issues/racial-justice/race-and-inequality-education/school-prison-pipeline

students who have been suspended multiple times." Students suspended or expelled for a discretionary violation are nearly three times more likely to enter the juvenile justice system the following year.[113]

In a radio interview with Big Boy TV, nineteen-year-old rapper Jaden Smith weighed in on the issue: 'We're preparing everybody to go through prison with the schools. There's too many correlations between public schools and prisons. The fact that you have the long hallways, the fact that you have a fixed responsibility to authority, the fact that there is a specific time to go outside and play, and there's a specific time you could come back in and the way that your notified by that happening is by the bells."[114]

Smith argues that the lack of jobs and additional educational and counseling services also contributes to America's growing prison population. He continues, stating that the US builds more prisons than schools.

Though an inaccurate statement, the United States does spend more on prisons than schools. It costs roughly three times as much to fund a prison as it does to fund a public

113 Ibid.

114 Random. (2018, June 6). *Jaden smith talking about the correlation between school and prison*[Video file]. Retrieved from https://www. youtube.com/watch?v=j6oiohWGzO8

school. Our judicial system has become one of the fastest growing marketplaces, bringing in billions of dollars per year.

* * *

It is apparent that the criminal justice system has no problem preying on the young, impressionable, and disenfranchised. Peter, a recovering addict who grew up in South Brooklyn, told me he learned "to be a victim of society" through his contact with the criminal justice system. "I fell right into that trap of doing drugs, getting arrested for crimes...,going into jail, going into court, instantly having a felony on my record. Now I can't get a job anywhere even though this happened, you know, over 15 years ago, I'm still considered and looked at as this person... everywhere I go because that›s what society has branded me."

Pete, now in recovery, says that his addiction to drugs and alcohol enabled him to fall victim to the system. Now, over a year sober, after many years in and out of the program, Pete leads one of my meetings in Philly on Tuesday nights. He says there were some benefits to spending time in rehab and jail, namely structure and schedule. Pete lacked discipline in those areas and he noted that once he reentered the community, he did need to be able to keep a schedule. "My schedule depends on other people's schedules...my job is my schedule...my kids, their school is my schedule."

However, Pete says his time institutionalized "caused [him] a lot of misplaced hatred, harm and victimization...I felt like a member of a fixed society." Pete's addiction to drugs and alcohol did put him in the position to be arrested. It placed him at risk to serve time at Spofford Juvenile Detention in the Bronx, and then Rikers Island. Judges continued to threaten him with these consequences, but his behavior did not change. He has multiple visits and stays at "central booking" in New York and later served time in the "Gun Club" County Jail in Florida.

"I was branded this type of person very young on so that I had no other choice. You can't take someone like that and then say, okay, now don›t do it again. That's all they know now."

Pete's story as an addict introduced to the criminal justice system at an early age makes an important point: if the criminal justice system is a profitable business, it would be beneficial to seek out the most vulnerable to imprison, children and those suffering from addiction.

What do jails and prisons do for addicts once incarcerated? Next to nothing.

If you are a heroin addict and not already on a maintenance drug regime using prescriptions such as methadone or suboxone, you're on your own. "Cold turkey bone dry sober," as Pete put it. "They might give you Adavan, Tramadol, or Remeron as any detox would but other than that, there's not a medical professional for that type of condition [withdrawal] in jail."

Alice, a recovering addict, experienced this struggle firsthand when she had to face the consequences of her past use. "I had criminal charges that I had accrued throughout the course of my using. I had stolen money from my coworkers and they charged me." She had a warrant for her arrest, but her lawyer told her she would be in and out of court.

That did not happen.

The judge raised her bail and she was taken out in handcuffs.

"It was a humiliating experience. It was awful," Alice told me. "I was worried I was going to go into withdrawal because I'm on Suboxone and they don't give you that in jail." Alice told me that recovering addicts on maintenance programs, such as Suboxone, are given Tylenol with Codeine or Klonopin in jail. "There's no research that says to detox a person off of heroin or opioids to use Tylenol with codeine and Klonopin." There isn't any research—Alice is right. However, as Pete explained to me, "Ff you come into the jail and you already have a script for [suboxone], the prison, by law, must find a doctor that could treat you because... they'll get medically sued for it." Luckily, Alice was bailed out in time and did not have to go through withdrawal, but she did spend one night in jail.

* * *

If the criminal justice system is profiting off young addicts, what does treatment look like in a juvenile detention center?

To find out, I asked Brian Fretwell. Brian worked in the long-term chemical addiction specific unit, where juvenile inmates worked a nine-month treatment program. A combination of positive peer culture and therapeutic community were the treatment modalities used in the juvenile program.

Brian admits he was "way too young and a little bit headstrong," but nevertheless he tried to make an impact on those kids.

Brian was twenty-two when he began teaching juvenile drug addicts, drug dealers, and gang members. He wanted to make a difference in his community. For the first few months, he felt he was making a difference. His students were doing well in class, they were progressing through their programs and were released.

Everything was going well, until Brian met Nathan.

Nathan was a fifteen-year-old methamphetamine addict. His gang tattoos, scars, and damaged teeth told the story of the life he had lived. What stood out to Brian was Nathan's honesty.

When it came time for Nathan to make a plan for when he got out of juvenile corrections, he was honest. As he looked Brian directly in the eye he said, "Mr. Fretwell, when I get back into the community, I'm going to continue using meth."[115]

Brian frantically tried to change his mind. Using graphs, charts, and statistics he tried to help Nathan see that he would continue to come back to custody or die, just as family and friends had before him.

However, the more Brian tried to convince Nathan, the less it seemed to matter to him.

As a teacher, Brian lived for the "aha" moments, when a student was able to understand something new. When it came to his future, Nathan didn't think he had anything to learn—nothing left for him to discover, nothing Brian could tell him that he didn't already know.

---

115 TEDx Talks. (2018, June 26). *What a 15-year-old meth addict taught me about leadership | Brian Fretwell | TEDxBoise*[Video file]. Retrieved from https://www.youtube.com/watch?v=qiN67V5q3C4

He understood the plan he was supposed to create, he just knew he wasn't going to follow through.

Brian says whether you are a manager, a teacher, a parent, or a friend, you've likely encountered this situation—you've told someone time and time again what to do, but they don't follow through.

He says it's almost naive to think an answer will change a behavior. If it were simply about having a solution to a problem, we could get everyone to quit smoking just by telling them it causes cancer.

As Brian continued to struggle with Nathan, a coworker named Sal asked him, "When is the last time you asked Nathan what he wants?" Brian said, "Thank you very much, but I know what Nathan wants, he wants to do meth."[116]

Sal told him there was an easier way: start with a question. He told Brian, "Every time you interact with Nathan, ask him a question. Every time you talk to Nathan, ask him a question. I want you to start with a question."[117]

---

116 Ibid.
117 Ibid.

Sal would approach Brian and ask, "Did you really ask a question there, or were you really just giving him the answers?"[118]

Brian almost gave up after a few weeks, but he noticed something. Nathan was uncomfortable. One time Brian asked him, "Nathan what do you want for your future?", and he responded, sarcastically, "I want a million dollars, I want to be president of the world."[119]

That sarcasm was a defense mechanism that was hiding something. Brian would ask, "Nathan, what is it that really matters to you?", to which Nathan would respond, "Mr. Fretwell, leave me alone! Stop asking me questions!"[120]

Nathan was frustrated, protecting something. He was protecting his hopes and dreams that had been battered and bruised. He still believed in himself, deep down.

Finally, Brian cornered Nathan and said, "You have to want more than this! Why are you lying to me! Why won't you be honest, and tell me what you really want."[121]

118 TEDx Talks. (2018, June 26). *What a 15-year-old meth addict taught me about leadership | Brian Fretwell | TEDxBoise*[Video file]. Retrieved from https://www.youtube.com/watch?v=qiN67V5q3C4
119 Ibid.
120 Ibid.
121 Ibid.

As Brian looked down, he saw Nathan's fist clench and his shoulders get tight. He started to quiver a bit.

As he looked up at Brian, Nathan said, "Mr. Fretwell, I don't want this! I don't want this life. I want to have a family. I want to be the first in my family to make something of this."[122]

In that moment, Brian didn't see a drug addict or a gang member. He saw the little kid that Nathan had been hiding inside himself likely for his whole life.

* * *

Brian and Nathan's story highlights a challenge that the judicial system grapples with daily: how to foster long-term recovery.

The threat of jail time will not keep an addict clean. However, placing offenders into treatment in place of custody provides the space to explore the underlying issues fueling their addiction.

Only the addicted individual can decide what to do with the opportunity to change. So long as that opportunity is available, recovery is possible.

---

122 Ibid.

CHAPTER SIX

ADDICTION AFFECTS US ALL

———

In July of 2018, I traveled to the Standing Rock Reservation in North Dakota with a church mission group.

Native American reservations have a long history of alcohol and drug abuse.

Pushed aside during the early years of our nation's formation, Native Americans still feel the pain of systematic and generational trauma.

Many families have long histories of substance abuse to cope with that trauma, and the teenagers we served at Camp Gabriel were already on the path I had found myself on not seven months before arriving in North Dakota. During these three days, I assisted young girls experiencing withdrawal while away from their supply. I listened to their stories of abuse, poverty, and hopelessness.

Why did these kids open up to me, a total stranger, who looked nothing like them and lived hundreds of miles away? Because I was vulnerable with them about my own experience.

After speaking on a panel the second day of camp, I was approached by many of our campers just wanting to share their stories with me. We had many of the same experiences and found many commonalities in the reasons we drank and used.

* * *

After the trip, I followed up with Bobby Grey Eagle, a minister who grew up on the reservation with the kids we served in July. Bobby told me about his community and their inability to address their historical trauma.

"It's an issue," Bobby told me. "From all the way up on our tribal council, there's this pain." The children on the reservation don't want to go to school; they stay at home. Staying at home, however, Bobby tells me puts the children at risk to be emotionally, physically, or sexually abused. "There's no hope down here," Bobby tells me, a truth I witnessed by spending time with the children at Camp Gabriel.

Communities such as the people of Standing Rock lack mental health resources; this lack inhibits those struggling from finding the help they need. Therefore, they find drugs and alcohol to manage their emotional pain.

"The problem is that we don't know who we are," Bobby told me. "I think that the historical trauma is so far reaching that it disconnects spirituality from every area of our life and we've forgotten who we are." Bobby told me it is a common understanding in his community that if their "children are going to succeed in this world, and then they have to start acting white."

Bobby's mother explained to him that they stopped teaching the language; they stopped teaching their children about their culture "because they thought that was the way for the children to succeed in this new world, in this new environment"

Bobby is a recovering alcoholic himself. "I wasn't ready to quit drinking. I had to." He believes the community must come together and be of service to one another. He says that if a woman is taking care of her six grandchildren and can't handle it, her neighbors must find a way to help her make meals throughout the day. "That's the level of community we got to get back to. I'm not saying we have to go back to the old way, but right now it's worse on the [Reservation] because we don't have the resources."

* * *

According to the American Psychological Association, among Native American adolescents between the ages of twelve and seventeen, rates of the use of cigarettes, at 16.8 percent compared to 10.2 percent, marijuana, at 13.8 percent compared to 6.9, and nonmedical uses of prescription drugs, at 6.1 percent compared to 3.3 percent are higher compared to the national average.[123]

Why are so many Native youths using drugs?

As Bobby told me, the young people on Standing Rock struggle with a wide variety of mental health challenges, which have resulted in a startling amount of suicides.

In fact, according to SAMHSA, suicide is the second leading cause of death—2.5 times the national rate—for Native male youth aged fifteen to twenty-four.

---

123 Ethnicity and Health in America Series: Substance Abuse/Addiction in Native American Youth. (n.d.). *American Psychological Association*. Retrieved from https://www.apa.org/pi/oema/resources/ethnicity-health/native-american/substance-use

* * *

Religious institutions, such as churches, synagogues, and temples, are often the first place people go when they are struggling. However, those who suffer from mental illness and addiction face harsh stigmas that keep them away from support, treatment, and understanding.

When it comes to addiction, many who are religiously affiliated hope that all the answers are in the church, their temple, or their synagogue. "Not true," says Reverend Bobby Grey Eagle. He argues from his position in the church that meetings and programs were created because "the church hadn't stepped up." These groups, Bobby continued to tell me, understand "confidentiality better than we do. We're not doing a good enough job talking about it and everybody just keeps on pushing it under the rug."

Gail M, whom I lovingly call my recovery mom, tells me she has faced similar challenges as a member of the Jewish faith. She recalls returning from rehab and her former party friends from synagogue "put up a wall," worried they would "catch [her] disease." Despite receiving letters from her rabbi while in treatment, Gail still felt isolated.

"I think a lot of it is because people don't know what to say." She explains that, like any disease, people may not be comfortable discussing it. However, addiction stands apart from other diseases because it is plagued by skepticism and stigma that it is a moral issue. "I just don't think there›s enough education in churches and synagogues," Gail tells me.

* * *

While at Standing Rock, I was able to talk with the kids we served as well as the adults who were doing their best to support the community.

"Problematic patterns of substance use are often linked to early initiation of use." The Native American youth is disproportionately affected by addiction.[124]

Native Americans are incarcerated at a rate 38 percent higher than the national average, according to the Bureau of Justice Statistics.

After leaving the reservation, I kept in touch with a few of the kids I met there. A fifteen-year-old girl and I became close. We spent many nights talking about our shared experiences.

---

124 Ethnicity and Health in America Series: Substance Abuse/Addiction in Native American Youth. (n.d.). *American Psychological Association*. Retrieved from https://www.apa.org/pi/oema/resources/ethnicity-health/native-american/substance-use

She was heavily withdrawing throughout camp and was having trouble eating and engaging with her peers. We spent long nights talking, and I left her with one piece of advice. I did not push her to get sober or to get treatment, but told her to stick to weed and avoid harder drugs.

A few months later she told me she had tried smoking meth, which landed her into treatment. We talked on the phone while she was in rehab and I told her it was good that she was given this chance so young.

Not long after, she told me she had "caught a case" and was now on probation. It was for a fight with another girl. Probation is difficult to navigate, especially for a sixteen-year-old girl with a lack of family stability.

* * *

Another camper I met revealed to me that he was queer, but was unable to come out to his family or community. Many cultures and families inhibit teens from being their authentic selves, which often leads to emotional and mental disorders, including addiction.

According to SAMHSA, "sexual minorities (e.g., people who identify as lesbian, gay, bisexual, or transgender) are at greater risk for substance use and mental health issues."[125]

Due to the unusual amount of stress, anxiety, and depression that members of the LGBTQ+ community face, they often turn to drugs and alcohol to cope.

Sexual minorities are often subjected to a form of repression that other minorities do not experience. If a person is female or African American, they will likely encounter bigotry at several points in their lifetime; however, they never have to *tell* anyone that they are a member of a less privileged demographic.

There is no fear of "coming out," because everyone already knows who they are.

The hypothetical closet is essentially a dilemma, a mandatory ultimatum in which members of the LGBTQ+ community must either decide to either suffer persecution and

---

125 Medley, G., Lipari, R. N., Bose, J., Cribb, D. S., Kroutil, L. A., & McHenry, G. (2015). Sexual Orientation and Estimates of Adult Substance Use and Mental Health: Results from the 2015 National Survey on Drug Use and Health. Retrieved from SAMHSA website: https://www.samhsa.gov/data/sites/default/files/NSDUH-SexualO-rientation-2015/NSDUH-SexualOrientation-2015/NSDUH-Sexual-Orientation-2015.htm

possibly physical violence or else keep living in a cage of conscious denial.

According to the Suicide Prevention Resource Center, between 5 and 10 percent of LGBTQ+ youth have attempted suicide, a rate 1.5 to three times higher than that of heterosexual youth.

It is not unlikely for kids on the reservation between the ages of fifteen and eighteen to face challenges with addiction, incarceration, teen pregnancy, and suicide.

However, Native Americans are largely left out of the addiction debate. Today, in 2019, the debate has changed.

* * *

Addiction today is considered a disease. However, for too many years, addiction was seen as a crime.

We have made great progress in moving toward treatment rather than incarceration. The uncomfortable truth is this change is largely influenced by who's getting addicted.

Before the prescription painkiller epidemic, many Americans wrongly thought drugs such as heroin were only a problem for communities of color. In 2001, 45 percent of Americans supported tough on crime drug laws, according to a 2012 study done by the Pew Research Center.[126]

The federal government spent $6.7 billion dollars on law enforcement in 2003, which disproportionately locks up people of color.[127]

Today, the opioid crisis is hitting white and Native Americans hard. White and Native American people have the highest rate of deaths from opioids. When white people are suffering from an addiction, it's a disease, not a crime.

As of 2015, two out of three Americans support treatment over punishment. The federal government now spends more money on treatment—$14.3 billion—than law enforcement—$9.5 billion.[128]

Regardless of the racial motivations behind this shift in perception, change is necessary to save lives and support the recovery community.

* * *

126 MTV. (2016, October 11). *Prescription for Change: Ending America's Opioid Crisis*[Video file]. Retrieved from https://www.youtube.com/watch?v=2QePuumO310
127 Ibid.
128 Ibid.

Yvonne's story is featured in the 2016 MTV documentary, "Prescription for Change." Yvonne has lived on a reservation her whole life.[129]

"I would say I was about 12 when pills hit," she says. "It just took a toll on the tribe."

She says the first time she smoked heroin was with her dad. At the time, Yvonne was using Vicodin and Percocet, but her dad convinced her the heroin was "twenty times better and twenty times cheaper" than the pills.

"I was dumb and I was gullible and I was dope sick," she says. "I was withdrawing so bad that I was like okay whatever and once I took that first hit, there was no going back."

Yvonne goes to behavioral health with the tribe, which the tribe pays for. In a conversation with her chemical dependency counselor, Brianna, Yvonne says she "doesn't know how to cope yet." Brianna, who is six years clean, reminds her "we're never fixed."

Sitting in a meeting, Yvonne says she started using opiates right after she had her daughter. She was just about to turn

---

129 MTV. (2016, October 11). *Prescription for Change: Ending America's Opioid Crisis*[Video file]. Retrieved from https://www.youtube.com/watch?v=2QePuumO310

eighteen. Her daughter was taken from her a year later. She got clean from coming out of jail and regained custody of her four-year-old daughter.

Yvonne says that even though she-s been clean off heroin for fifteen months, her daughter still worries she's going to leave again. She says, "I'm grateful to wake up in the morning to listen to my four-year-old daughter wake me up."

* * *

A large part of recovery is carrying the message through acts of service—bringing the solution we have found to those who still suffer. I believe my sobriety and my life today is my testimony.

Each one of us at Camp Gabriel this July, the adult leaders— the campers, and youth counselors—held our own testimony, whether we were aware of it or not. It is no coincidence we were all gathered together.

Before we left on our trip, we played a few rounds of speed dating, asking each other a few get to know you questions. One question I enjoyed answering was "What is your life mantra?" Mine is "walk in love." We are to spread love and extend our hand to each and everyone we meet. That was clear to me while on the Standing Rock reservation. Whatever

I gave to that camp and those people, it was returned to me tenfold by means of their hospitality, vulnerability, and unconditional love.

All ten of us who traveled to North Dakota had our own personal experience, but I think a common thread throughout was love, and to me, that is what we are called to do: to love.

CHAPTER SEVEN

RECOVERY IS POSSIBLE

———

Had I not been fortunate enough to have the support and care in my parents' home, I would have gone to treatment at the Caron Foundation in Wernersville, Pennsylvania.

The Caron Foundation is an internationally recognized nonprofit foundation, with treatment centers in Texas, Florida, and Pennsylvania. The Caron Foundation began when its founder, Richard Caron, used his home as a retreat for those in recovery. Eventually, he purchased a hotel on a farm in Pennsylvania and opened what is now one of the most successful treatment centers in the nation.

The Caron Foundation uses a comprehensive approach to treatment and works with top university medical centers to further the efficacy of certain treatment methods. Caron centers its program on the twelve-step method, but also has a unique relapse program.

"At Caron, teens and young adults are in treatment together because many of their core issues are similar...Teens are encouraged to develop their sense of responsibility as they progress through treatment through the use of 'recovery stages.' Each of the three stages requires that the teen meet established clinical and behavioral benchmarks. As patients progress through the stages, they receive incentives and are given additional responsibilities, such as taking on a leadership role or mentoring newer patients, which gives them a sense of pride and bolsters their self-esteem."[130]

* * *

When Gail entered treatment at the Caron Foundation, she was the only opiate addict in her group. "No one knew what opiate withdrawal looked like," Gail told me. "They all thought I was crazy."

Gail was crying, shaking, and in pain due to the amount of prescription drugs she had been abusing, including opiates and antidepressants.

---

130 Young Adult Addiction Rehab (Pennsylvania Campus). (n.d.). Retrieved from Caron Foundation website: https://www.caron.org/our-programs/inpatient-treatment/young-adults

Gail described rehab as a "glorified hospital." She committed to getting better for her family and for the first time she did not want any mood altering substances.

Caron also offers programming for the family of the recovering alcoholic or addict.

At Caron, "treating the whole family is critical." Family members are brought into the admission and assessment process from the start, so that "their input can form the basis for a personalized addiction treatment plan."

At Caron Renaissance's extended-stay program, new families are paired with an alumni family "buddy" who can provide support, answer questions, and share experiences.

* * *

Alice has spent time in multiple recovery facilities.

"My first experience was just awful. It was because of the particular facility that I was at. I just felt like it was a zoo. So I only stayed for four days. I only stayed for detox and then I signed out AMA [against medical advice] because I was so uncomfortable."

The second time Alice was sent to treatment was because her work as a nurse and stealing drugs left the State Board of Nursing no choice but to give her an ultimatum.

She said her second rehab experience was better. "I felt like they had a good program and that they cared about their patients. It was structured, very structured."

A typical day in rehab, as Alice described, was almost like school. They were up by seven, and had group therapy and meetings with breaks in between.

"They were really long days...I needed that structure...because when you›re out there you just sleep, you don't eat, you don›t do anything that's healthy."

Unfortunately, Alice could only stay for two weeks because her insurance "kicked her out." They were willing to pay for an intensive outpatient stay, which was five days a week for six hours each day, followed by general outpatient, which was two days a week. Alice wasn›t working at the time and the $50 co-pay each day was too much. She did the intensive outpatient for as long as she could afford it.

"I still wasn't ready," Alice told me. "I was going through a divorce and then gotten into a relationship that was very toxic and abusive...the cycle just started all over again. But by the time I was ready to go into treatment for the third time, it was my own, like I was ready to go. I was willing to go."

At this point, Alice had welfare insurance, which allowed her to get right into treatment without deductibles or co-pays, which she had to deal with when she had private insurance. She stayed twenty days.

"I take Suboxone every day, but I realized that that alone will not keep you sober,. I needed a program of recovery and I had to do it."

* * *

Returning to the real world following treatment can be hard. Transitional living or halfway houses can be a great option. A sober house provides an environment of entirely of sober people, who can go to meetings together, and share the same goal.

When James left rehab, he thought he would return to his parents house to live in the same environment he did when he was using. However, his rehab convinced his parents to sign a three-month contract with a sober house.

"At the sober house I was more depressed than I had ever been before," James said, "I was not ready to live on my own anywhere."

James went to a second transitional living facility and celebrated a year of sobriety there. "As soon as I got to Strathmore, my depression turned around greatly. That's what's lead to me living here for so long. I'm happy here. Being able to live in a sober house lets me be more immersed in recovery. I would definitely recommend sober living to others. It makes it so you can't forget you're in recovery. Constantly seeing new, broken people coming in makes you remember how bad it was. While, at the same time, seeing people further ahead of you shows where you could be if you continue your path. I've been at Strathmore for 9 months, another sober house for 3 months and I would not change anything about the path I've taken."

For James, transitional living has greatly benefitted his sobriety, but it came at a cost. His first sober house cost $8,000 a month and his current house, $6,500 a month.

"It's not cheap," James said, "but they both offer case managers and weekly meetings to see where you are. They offer motivation and help to achieve your goals. Most sober houses that are $600 to $1,100 a month have much less support and require you to do most of the work on your own."

* * *

The Hazelden Betty Ford Foundation, a leading addiction treatment and advocacy organization in the field, has called for reform in the addiction treatment industry.

"From misleading sales tactics, deceptive advertising and unethical marketing practices to healthcare insurance fraud and patient brokering, the largely unregulated field of drug rehab is rife with deceptive and unscrupulous—even illegal—business activities."[131]

The opioid crisis has driven a growing market demand for addiction treatment. The specialized addiction treatment industry is now a $35 billion industry. In 2003, it was only $21 billion, and it is expected to top $42 billion by 2020.

As a leading member of the National Association of Addiction Treatment Providers, the Hazelden Betty Ford Foundation "is committed to a robust code of ethics, and their Recovery Advocacy team is focused on addressing the following unethical and dangerous emerging business trends in the industry,"[132] such as excessive consumer billing, insurance fraud, deceptive marketing, and patient brokering.

---

131 Reforming the Addiction Treatment Industry. (n.d.). Retrieved from Hazelden Betty Ford Foundation website: https://www.hazeldenbettyford.org/recovery-advocacy/reforming-addiction-treatment-industry

132 Ibid.

Betty Ford says "it is time to restore faith and accountability in the addiction treatment field. It is time to establish quality standards and an enforceable regulatory framework to guide all treatment organizations. It is time to ensure ethical, quality care for all people who seek help for addiction."[133]

* * *

Though I did not attend treatment, I have visited rehabs in both Philadelphia and Boston. My twelve-step program is built upon service and carrying a message of recovery. I have been fortunate enough to go on "commitments" to multiple rehabs and sober living facilities throughout my sobriety.

My first commitment was at a halfway house in Boston called Hope House. I was only four months sober and skeptical that I would be of any service to anyone else. My sponsor suggested I go, so a group of recovering alcoholics and I carpooled to the house, talking about our own experiences on the drive there.

The drive to meetings or commitments is often called "the meeting before the meeting." The time I spend with other

---

133 Reforming the Addiction Treatment Industry. (n.d.). Retrieved from Hazelden Betty Ford Foundation website: https://www.hazeldenbettyford.org/recovery-advocacy/reforming-addiction-treatment-industry

recovering alcoholics is essential to my recovery. It is during this time that I am able to make friends and connections with others in the recovery community.

When we arrived at Hope House, the five of us shared our experience, strength, and hope with the residents. I love sharing my story at rehabs and sober houses. I have been taught by my fellow alcoholics that I have a unique message to give to the people around me. Even if my story does not resonate with the majority of the room, one person might walk away with the strength they need to stay sober that day from something I said.

It also benefits my recovery to go on commitments to get out of myself and be of service to someone else. Since that first commitment, I have chased down opportunities to be of service to others. Speaking in both Boston and Philadelphia, I have learned that you can only maintain your sobriety by giving it away. Being of service to others is paramount to long-term recovery.

Service is not limited to going on commitments. I was taught that service can be as simple as making coffee before the meeting, or giving your phone number to someone in their first few weeks of sobriety.

To me, service means giving away what was so freely given to me. When I was at my lowest, strong, sober women gave me their phone number, they took me to meetings and they helped me see what a sober life could look like.

My recovery has been built by the women around me. By taking their suggestions, even when I didn't want to, I have been able to shed the anger, self-pity, and grief that I came into the rooms with. These feelings will continue to come back and drive me to drink if I do not continue to follow the path of the women before me.

It is now my responsibility to lead other women on that path, and I have done so to the best of my ability. Sponsorship is something that is sacred in the program. I have often been told to stay in the middle of the program by having a sponsor and being a sponsor to others. I have been lucky enough to sponsor two recovering alcoholics, one fifteen-year-old and one eighteen-year-old. It has been one of the greatest pleasures of my life.

* * *

Recovery is not linear. It is a slow process and hard work. I have found that staying honest, open-minded, and willing allows me to continue to move forward. Times where I have been stubborn and clung to my old ways have put me in a rut, feeling miserable once again. Therefore, I must move forward and use the tools I have available to me.

My therapist has reminded me over the four years we have worked together that "the caterpillar does not just wake up one day and become a butterfly." I cannot change overnight, either, but luckily I have a lifetime to build a beautiful life for myself.

CHAPTER EIGHT

NEVER HAD A
LEGAL DRINK

———

Across America, colleges and universities are adding a new feature to their admissions brochures: recovery programs for students afflicted with the diseases of alcoholism and addiction.

As I approached six months of sobriety, I began dutifully researching and connecting with recovery program directors at schools across the country, including the University of Connecticut, Brown University, The University of Vermont, Rutgers University, and the Pennsylvania State University, to name a few.

What intrigued me about recovery programs in higher education was not my own personal interest or need for such services at my college, but the lack of awareness that these programs existed.

Most college campuses have begun to address drugs and alcohol through prevention counseling. Many, however, have stopped there, lacking the education and resources to take the next steps to treatment and recovery. Through my research, I have learned that recovery programs in higher education are not only necessary to holistically serve a student body, but are a powerful example of strength on college campuses.

* * *

Prevention, treatment, and recovery. For years, institutions of higher education have focused their budgets into prevention offices; however, students are not getting the help they need. Universities should not, in my opinion, take on the responsibility of treatment, but they need to be equipped to refer students to external care providers as well as able to welcome students in recovery back into their community.

I was given the option of going to rehab; however, I chose to dive headfirst into a twelve-step program. I didn't realize how hard it would be to seamlessly return to classes after only taking two months off. The transition process back to campus after treatment or time off is never easy, but universities that place an emphasis on assisting students in recovery have been able to provide continuing care for students coming back to college.

Recovery programs, though seemingly few, are widespread on many college campuses. The lack of knowledge of such programs makes it difficult for universities to establish and embrace communities of recovery. In an age of binge drinking and social drug use, many students dismiss the idea of having a "fatal disease" such as alcoholism or addiction. In reality, 49 percent of nineteen to twenty-two year old college students use marijuana daily, the highest level in this age group since the early 1980s. Thirty-two percent of college students have engaged in binge drinking—more the five drinks—in the past two weeks, according to a DrugAbuse. Gov 2016 Study.

The likelihood of college students living with alcoholism or addiction without knowing it is high considering the environment they are living in. The American Medical Association (AMA) declared that alcoholism was an illness in 1956, but many still consider the disease a choice, hindering acceptance and understanding of those in recovery. With 10 percent of people in recovery being under thirty, college campuses are the ideal place for this education, awareness, and programming to start.

* * *

After talking to many recovery program directors, I learned there is no one right way of providing services to students in recovery. Many of the program directors came from backgrounds of being alcoholics or addicts themselves, while others were champions for the cause. Many recovery programs in higher education provide programming, but a large part of recovery on campus is substance free housing.

Housing at the institutions I spoke to is generally open to students pursuing recovery, with a minimum of ninety days of recovery. Substance free living offers students a chance to enjoy college without isolating themselves to avoid relapse. Students living in sober houses across the country work their own programs, whether that be twelve-step programs or other legitimate programs of recovery. In addition to sub-free housing, programming such as weekly check in meetings, leadership workshops and community retreats are commonly a part of recovery programs.

I felt inspired as I listened to the stories of how these programs came to life—I could sense the passion of the students. The programs grew organically. Yes, the rate of growth was frustrating, but the students continued to build their program and their communities. Many programs that focus on substance abuse have also opened their doors with an all recovery lens, welcoming students struggling with mental illness, eating disorders, survivors of suicide, self-harm, abuse, assault, and students in their own recovery as the friends and family members of alcoholics. An all-recovery approach has not worked for all colleges, but institutions like Texas Tech University and The George Washington University have found great success in including students in a wide variety of recovery.

Though programs of recovery have been instituted on college campuses nationally, difficulties have arisen with college policies and administrative values. Many program directors have expressed their frustration with college policy as it relates to their students in recovery. Many students have faces expulsion and suspension even after they have sought recovery on campus. Unconscious bias toward students of color, low income and first generation students has been a continuous point of contention between campus police and judicial staff on many college campuses. Program directors have expressed their need for their own universities to publicly support the efforts toward recovery on campus, although many are hesitant to market the idea.

Educating the student body, campus police, judicial staff, class deans, residential life, counseling ,and health centers is a great start, but including high level administrators in the conversation is the key to establishing collegiate recovery programs as an important part of student life.

* * *

The Association of Recovery in Higher Education's (ARHE) Northeast Regional Representative Anne Heller taught me that there is nothing more important and valuable than sharing our own experiences. Education as a whole isn't just learning to read and write; it is learning who you are and how you can be of service to those around you. My recovery journey came from a place of deep discontent with my life. Being a voice of hope and love on my own campus is a small way I can show my gratitude.

Collegiate programs of recovery are on the rise across the country; my college will be joining the hundreds of institutions already serving students in recovery. After a year of research, working with administration, and sheer persistence, I was able to help create a substance free floor through residential life. Students applied to live in the space, thoughtfully answering questions about their interest in the housing and what they would bring to the community. My hope is that as institutions of learning, colleges and universities will accept the idea of recovery as part of an education, beginning a dialogue our country desperately needs.

* * *

I've often heard people say, "*It's not alcoholism until you graduate.*"

It is. This excuse is one I used repeatedly.

"*But I'm too young to be an alcoholic.*"

"*I'm in college, this is normal.*"

"*Everyone drinks like me.*"

They didn't drink like me, and it wasn't normal. I don't remember a single time I drank without getting drunk.

It wasn't for lack of trying. I tried every method in the book: attempting to limit myself to two drinks, only drinking beer, only drinking on the weekend, only drinking with friends, and so on. When I drank, I couldn't stop drinking. I have come to realize that I cannot drink like other people, as hard as I may try.

I have a disease of the body and mind. Mentally, I am constantly thinking of the next drink. Where am I going to get it? When am I going to be able to drink next? Who can I manipulate into getting me what I want? This thinking is what is commonly referred to as a mental obsession. Physically, I experience craving. When I have one drink, I want another, and another, and another, and another, until the bottle is empty. Even then, I want more.

It's never enough.

Binge drinking is a phenomenon that has become quite popular on college campuses. The prospect of getting wasted on the weekend after a long week of studying is understandably appealing to students. However, it can make it easy for potential or real alcoholics to hide among their peers.

This culture normalizes behaviors that would generally be considered alcoholic. Blackouts, vomiting, injuries, and chaos accompanied every single time I drank—these are not normal. Nonalcoholics can enjoy a few drinks and have a good time. For alcoholics, the goal is to get obliterated. The frat party, beer pong, keg stand nonsense perpetuates a culture that is dangerous for those college age kids passing off their alcoholism as being "*the life of the party.*"

I can't say for sure if I was born with the disease of addiction, but I can say that I always had the characteristics of an alcoholic, even before I picked up a drink. I was restless, irritable, and discontent. I felt out of place and uncomfortable in my own skin. However, as soon as I put a drink to my lips, that discomfort faded away. Suddenly, I was the prettiest, smartest, funniest girl in the room. This experience proves to me that alcohol and drugs are not my problem; sobriety is my problem. I am fundamentally uncomfortable living in my own body, and I needed an escape from myself. Alcohol and drugs did that for me.

The college culture of rewarding yourself for finishing a long week or getting through finals is great for nonalcoholics, but I never needed a reason to drink.

When I first got sober, it seemed like everyone couldn't help themselves from commending me on my strength at the age of eighteen. Every time I was told just how "lucky" I was, I wanted to respond by saying "F--k you, I'm in college, you really think I want to be hanging out with you people?" As time went on and I stopped counting the days, and reached a year without drugs and alcohol, I realized I was lucky.

* * *

A little over a year into my sobriety, I returned to a meeting in Natick, Massachusetts, that I had not been to in a few months.

Chairing and speaking at the meeting that night was a guy named Reuben.

As he told his story, I identified. Following the meeting he rushed up to me, "You're nineteen, right!?" I nodded. "I've been looking for people my age in the program!" I greeted him with a hug. We young people in the program tend to stick together, understanding that we need each other to survive.

Reuben became something like a brother to me in recovery. Hanging out, telling stories, and going to meetings together became a routine. As our friendship grew, I learned more about him that I hadn't known from the first time I heard his story in Natick.

Reuben grew up in Holliston, Massachusetts, the child of two very loving Jewish parents and a sister two years older. Though he attended preschool at his temple, he didn't consider his family religious. He spent his early childhood education in a French immersion program, and was practically fluent in the language by the end of kindergarten.

Reuben remembers at this age being prone to lying, recalling an incident in a department store when he stole a bracelet. "I remember I put it in my pocket and [my dad] asked me if I took it. I was like, no, and that's rare for a young kid to just straight up lie to his father." Eventually, he had to go back and return the bracelet to the store, in addition to sweeping up the office as punishment. "You'd think it would teach me a lesson with stealing and lying," Reuben told me, "but it didn't."

In first grade, Reuben's maternal grandfather passed away. His passing was Reuben's first exposure to death; he was six years old. Not a year later, one of his closest friends from school was diagnosed with leukemia. "I had no idea what that was." Reuben recalls nurses from the children's hospital coming in and explaining cancer to his second grade class. Throughout his friend's treatment, Reuben visited with gifts, specifically Webkinz, which I also remember as being popular at the time. He passed away two years later when Reuben was in the fourth grade.

"It was hard, you know, we [were] little kids." Reuben was nine.

A year later, his paternal grandfather passed away. "It's kinda sad thinking back because I do miss him...but I was really happy to be off school and that's where my...sick thinking [comes] in, and I was really pretty used to death."

Not a year later, Reuben's older sister started having extreme headaches, and they found a tumor in her brain. It was in sixth grade that Reuben smoked weed for the first time. He had been bugging a friend of his to smoke with him, so they went out to his friend›s house to do so. A "twenty-year-old dude" pulled up and handed the two young boys a paper bag and "a twenty bag." They went up to the bathroom and Reuben's friend, at the age of eleven, rolled a perfect joint for the two of them to smoke.

"I got so high, and you know what? I didn't like it that much," Reuben recalled. "I liked the feeling of not knowing what was going on and just kind of the escape. But I was uncomfortable because I was young and I was like, what the hell is going on?"

However, "the crazy thing" was that he wanted more.

He also drank that night, stealing bourbon and whiskey from his dad.

"My parents never drank. I've seen my dad drunk in my life twice. They smoked pot occasionally, but they weren't addicts." Reuben›s parents were self-proclaimed "dead heads;" that is, big fans of the band, the Grateful Dead. Smoking weed socially came with the territory of the concerts they frequented.

After drinking the stolen liquor, Reuben was "crossfaded"—drunk and high. This night was the first time he drank or smoked weed. "And that was kind of a pattern for a little bit," Reuben told me.

He had always struggled with his anger, once punching a kid at camp straight in the face for not liking his shirt. Now diagnosed with bipolar disorder, Reuben recalls his outbursts starting at a very young age. He was put in therapy and given a medication for Ritalin. Now a middle schooler smoking weed with older high school kids, Reuben was encouraged to crush and snort his Ritalin medication. "So I tried it. I remember the first time I didn't crush it up and my nose bled," he told me.

At this point in Reuben's life, his sister was undergoing surgery to remove the tumor in her brain. "After she got out of ICU...she was screaming. I didn't go in the room yet. She was screaming and crying. She wanted to go the bathroom by herself, but she couldn't. It was really sad. And I cried and then I walked away."

Reuben had to watch his sister learn to walk, talk, and function again. She still has chronic headaches and chronic fatigue to this day. She graduated college this year; Reuben was invited to her graduation. I noticed the way he lit up when he talked about his sister.

Continuing to smoke and drink with his new friends, his parents started to notice a lack of emotion, which led him to his first institution, a partial hospital program for mental illness. He ended up in a lockdown facility, which later was shut down for corruption.

"I was just so bad... I don't think I was withdrawing at all, but I think I was having a mental withdrawal." This was Reuben's first stint of sobriety.

He got out of the facility early after breaking his collarbone during a game of tackle football. After complaining about the pain at his bar mitzvah, a family friend offered him a Vicodin. He was thirteen years old, celebrating his bar mitzvah and drinking on Vicodin. Nobody thought anything of it.

He started selling pot that same year.

Come eighth grade, he was ripping people off and only hung out with his older friends. "I don't remember most of eighth grade honestly, which is pretty scary." Entering high school, Reuben was regularly smoking weed and cigarettes. "I wasn't drinking as much, but I was experimenting with pills, mostly benzos." He started hanging out with an older kid who was already deeply invested in substances. The boys would hang out after school and on the weekends, smoking pot and drinking heavily.

Reuben trusted this boy—they were friends—but he became physically and verbally abusive toward Reuben when he was under the influence. The last time the two hung out, Reuben drank enough to suffer from alcohol poisoning. "The first thing he did was punch me square in the face...he beat the shit out of me for real and he got my other friend to as well...I felt like I could trust them and I didn›t know any better." The boys threw Reuben out into the rain, left to call his parents for help. They picked him up and took him to the hospital where he was hooked up to an IV.

Like any alcoholic, this incident didn't deter Reuben from continuing to drink the way he did.

By his sophomore year in high school, Reuben had been placed in a support class for ‹trouble makers.› Unfortunately, his abusive ex-friend was also in the class. "I was having so much anxiety, I couldn›t handle myself." After getting into a fight with one of his classmates, he was suspended. This wasn›t his first suspension but it did lead to him leaving school to go to an alternative school.

During that time, Reuben dated a girl who introduced him to opiates and benzodiazepines, specifically Xanax. He soon left the alternative school and was sent to a behavioral school. "My anger was so bad," Reuben told me. "I threw a desk and just cursed out a teacher, you know, whatever...you could get suspended multiple times." He sold there and used there, especially acid.

That summer, he went on a trip to Israel through his camp, a place he had already been kicked out of twice. He vowed this time he would be good; he wouldn't disappoint everyone again. However, despite his determination to behave, he was caught drinking on the trip and was kicked out, again.

After the trip, he experienced his first run with an eating disorder—starving himself, he felt good about the way his skin hung on his bones.

Senior year of high school he used cocaine regularly, especially on the weekends.

Graduating high school was the beginning of the end for Reuben. He spent the majority of the summer after graduation selling drugs, constantly fielding questions from his parents about where all the money was coming from. He started community college and worked full time, but within three months he was institutionalized again.

"A lot of people didn't want to hang out with me anymore. I was just depressed, suicidal." Reuben remembers telling his parents he was going to get high before they took him to the psych ward. He stayed for five days and got high immediately after. "I was going nowhere...I just wasn't high anymore. I did what I could, stealing Adderall, Oxy, whatever I could find from my friends' cabinets, my family's cabinets. It was fucked up. I stole money from everyone for years," Reuben told me.

It was in that psych ward that Reuben met Justin, the first guy to take him to a twelve-step meeting, named "Tough Shit Don't Drink"—a men's meeting on Monday nights that Reuben still goes to this day.

Though Reuben was strung out at his first few meetings, he was given a sponsor. "Now I didn't know what the fuck that was," Reuben remembers, "I didn't know what the twelve steps were. I did get the idea that it wasn't a religious program and that did make me more comfortable because I've been an atheist for a long time."

He ended up relapsing, citing cocaine as one of the most difficult drugs to quit due to the mental obsession. "I was just always angry...trying to intimidate my parents, yelling at them, freaking out, punching walls...just destroying everything. And fucking disappointing everyone again."

Reuben's parents eventually kicked him out and he stayed at a respite for adults with severe mental health issues.

At this point, Reuben was eighteen years old and running out of options.

One night, "dosed out of [his] mind" on acid, cocaine, and Xanax, among other drugs, he got a call from his grandmother who told him he could come to live with her in Florida. It was in Florida that he had his first experience with withdrawals. "I felt sick, very sick." He had no options left; he had to go to a meeting.

Afterward, he connected with another man in the room by asking to bum a cigarette. The man introduced Reuben to his friends and brought him to his home group. "I kept going back every night," Reuben told me. He was working—selling insurance and waiting tables at Texas Roadhouse, where he met the sponsor he would work with during his time in Florida.

Reuben started a pattern in Florida, relapse after relapse, but he kept coming back. "It was the shuffle, really. I was just going back and forth," he told me. His eating disorder began to flare up again, and after talking to his mom on the phone and hearing a woman speak about her eating disorder, in a meeting, Reuben entered treatment.

"It was my first real rehab I'd ever been to." However, so many of the patients were still using that Reuben was accidentally exposed to fentanyl, which had been cut into the acid he did in treatment. He failed his drug test and was kicked out.

Following his stint in rehab, Reuben stayed with a girl and her family. They were all hardcore addicts. "I went the hardest I've ever gone in my life," he told me. "I was doing a lot of blow and I remember I smoked crack." He was lying to everyone he was still in contact with and living "so dirty."

"This was the worst I'd ever been in my life. And it brought me to my knees so quickly...I had the gift of desperation."

Reuben called his old sponsor to tell him he was using again—
his sponsor knew.

As he was high on a cocktail of opiates, he started on his way
to pick up heroin.

Just then, he got a call from a friend in a meeting, who
immediately came and picked him up. Thank God he did
call, for Reuben was ready to shoot up heroin, after never
previously putting a needle in his arm.

"It progressed that quickly...it's not a joke."

He went back to rehab, then to IOP, then to a sober house.
Rueben's family had cut off communication with him.
However, yet another death in the family brought them back
together. "I showed up for the funeral; I could never show up
for anyone before...I saw my dad and talked to him for the
first time in a very long time."

He went back home to Massachusetts just in time to pick
up his ninety-day coin. He had a lapse in going to meetings
around the holidays, but the return of cravings scared
him back into the rooms. He now goes to several different
meetings a week. He has a sponsor and a connection to a
higher power. "I don›t preach. [The program] is attraction
rather than promotion."

* * *

When I first met Reuben, he didn't strike me as an angry person, though anger is a large part of his story.

"No matter what happens, I can get through it. I have people, I have connections, I have everything I need in my life and I'm so happy and so lucky to be where I am," he tells me.

Like me, Reuben is nineteen years old and sober. He hasn't picked up a drink or a drug in over ten months. He is also now one of my favorite people.

* * *

In the United States, there are countless kids like Reuben who were exposed to drugs at an early age, accelerating their addiction. In 2018, *Time* magazine reported on an unusual high school in Seattle, Washington, designed for teens with addiction.

Marquez Martinez got sober on November 15, 2016. Until then, he had used OxyContin, Xanax, and nearly every other drug he could get his hands on, and at one point was suspended from school for selling drugs. His parents sent him to an inpatient treatment center, then enrolled him in this unusual high school, Interagency at Queen Anne, or IQA.

Though skeptical at first, Martinez immediately "felt safe" there. The Seattle public school campus is designed for students learning to lead sober lives while earning their diplomas. The twenty students at IQA attend class, regularly meet with a counselor, and attend daily support group meetings based on twelve-step programs.[134]

First appearing in the 1970s, forty recovery schools now exist nationwide in states including Minnesota, Texas, and Massachusetts. "There has been a gap in adolescent treatment for many, many years," says Andy Fitch, cofounder of the Association of Recovery Schools and associate professor at Vanderbilt University. "The schools are one of the programs that fill in that gap."[135]

Eighty-five percent of recovery schools are public or receive public funding, while some are private or part of rehabs. According to Fitch, new sober schools are in the works in states including New York, Delaware, and Oregon. However, it isn't easy starting a school, let alone a sober school. Delaware faced difficulties as local school districts were unable to provide the $2 million needed to cover staff costs.

---

134 Gorman, A. (2019, January 23). Inside the Specialized 'Recovery' High Schools Designed Just for Teens With Addiction. *Time Magazine.* Retrieved from http://time.com/5509829/sober-high-school-addiction/

135 Ibid.

* * *

Nationally, illicit drug use among middle and high school students has reached record lows. Still, nearly one in five tenth graders reported using an illegal drug in the previous 30 days, according to the annual nationwide "Monitoring the Future" survey.

Many of the students at IQA come to the school straight from treatment programs to avoid temptation at traditional high schools. "There, people offer you drugs every day," said fifteen-year-old Coltrane Fisher, who regularly used heroin, cocaine, and other illegal drugs before coming to the school.[136]

The success of recovery high schools is partly due to the fact that the students are among sober peers, as well as teachers and counselors who all support their sobriety.

"Unless these kids get engaged with other young people in recovery, they don't stand a chance," said Seth Welch, a recovery support counselor at Interagency Queen Anne. "This becomes their new community."[137]

---

136 Ibid.
137 Gorman, A. (2019, January 23). Inside the Specialized 'Recovery' High Schools Designed Just for Teens With Addiction. *Time Magazine*. Retrieved from http://time.com/5509829/sober-high-school-addiction/

Students at the school sign a sobriety pledge and agree to random drug testing. They aren't kicked out for relapsing, but Welch, the support counselor, works to get them back into treatment if they begin actively using again.

Since the school opened, twenty-one students have graduated. Welch and the teachers help students plan for the future. Martinez, for example, will graduate this month and is taking community college courses.

For Coltrane Fisher, the cost was hitting rock bottom. He began smoking marijuana at age twelve and then moved on to other drugs. Last year, he stopped going to school and didn't come home for days on end.

"Nobody grows up thinking you are going to become an addict," he said. "It just happens."[138]

* * *

Once I learned drugs and alcohol could lead me to contemplating suicide, I realized the severity of the disease of addiction. I've often heard the only options for active addicts are jails, institutions, or death. It is a terrible reality, but it

---

138 Ibid.

is my reality and I know that any one of my friends could succumb to this fate.

I still remember picking up the phone to hear Reuben on the other line, crying uncontrollably.

He was seven and a half months sober and one of his best friends had overdosed and died.

"When Jake died, I was lost," Reuben told me. "It wasn't so much as wanting to get high, but feeling like eventually everybody leaves us, some earlier than others."

Jake had helped Reuben get into treatment in Florida. "He did everything for me, even when I was at my worst in treatment, he was always supportive."

In less than a month, Reuben lost two more friends to overdoses.

Remembering his friend, Reuben said, "He was just an amazing guy; he just couldn't love himself."

* * *

I'd like you to imagine slowly losing one of your loved ones.

Watching them lose their job, their family, their health.

Watching from the sidelines as they lose sight of their place in the world.

Watching their life grow smaller and smaller.

Though you try, you're unable to help them.

Now, I'd like you to imagine it is you losing.

Losing opportunities, friends, and purpose.

You want so badly to recover what you've lost, but it feels impossible to dig yourself out of the hole.

You're completely hopeless.

Take a breath.

Recovery is possible.

One day at a time.

I am living, breathing proof.

ACKNOWLEDGEMENTS1

When I decided to write Pregame, I had no idea what gifts were in store for me. Writing your truth and reading it back to yourself is nothing less than cathartic. I own who I am, and I can confidently say that after putting it all down in black and white. I urge everyone who may read this book to take ownership of your story; you are the only one that can tell you who you are.

Thank you to Eric Koester for convincing me I had a story to tell and the entire New Degree team for their constant support and patience. Thank you to Brian Bies and Heather Gomez for saving me from looking illiterate and reminding me that "it will get done." Thank you to the wonderful people who allowed me to share their stories in this project.

I am immensely grateful to the "village" that has raised me and continues to support me.

First to my family, thank you mom and dad for teaching me to be a resilient and hard working individual. The lessons you have instilled in me will continue to guide me throughout my life. To my not so little sister, Leslie, thank you for being my best friend. You are and always will be my favorite person on the planet. To Mira, thank you for saving my life. You are nothing but a bright light in my life and I thank God everyday for bringing us together. To Caitlyn, thank you for calling me every single day in my first year of sobriety. Your love and friendship is unmatched and I will always be grateful. To Sarah for sharing in some of the best and worst moments of my life, you've always been there. To Angela, for consistently telling the truth, whether I like it or not. And, to Claudia Trevor-Wright and the Wellesley Community (especially the Wellesley Field Hockey team) for welcoming me back with open arms and understanding hearts.

Most of all, thank you to the recovery communities of both the city of Philadelphia and the city of Boston. I am a better daughter, sister, friend, student, and woman because of your strength and your love. Recovery is hard work, but I know I'm never alone. From the bottom of my heart, thank you.

CPSIA information can be obtained
at www.ICGtesting.com
Printed in the USA
BVHW040322120719
553258BV00004B/5/P